"Many people have the view that Jesus was basically a friendly and warm teacher. Those who have read the Gospels closely recognize, though, that Jesus said and did things that upset this rosy portrait. *Jesus Behaving Badly* engages the hard 'sayings' and 'doings' of Jesus, not by merely explaining them away, but by representing a fullness of Jesus in the three dimensions of a real historical figure and in the fourfold portrayal of the Gospels. If the aim of this book is to reckon with the whole Jesus and not a mere caricature, Strauss has accomplished this with sense and wit."

Nijay K. Gupta, George Fox Evangelical Seminary

"We have rehabilitated Jesus so much today that we can't imagine how anyone wouldn't admire Jesus. How could anyone hate this lovable guy enough to scream, 'Crucify him!'? Yet, a fuller reading of the Gospels reveals a tree-hating, name-calling troublemaker who often didn't play well with others. Maybe the home crowd at Nazareth wanted to stone him because he was a 'stubborn and rebellious son' (Deut 21:18-21). Yet, in a delightfully written book, Strauss treats fairly these typical objections to Jesus and guides the reader to a fuller understanding of this complex man from Galilee. Anyone wanting to understand Jesus better, whether in a classroom or Bible study, should read this book."

E. Randolph Richards, Palm Beach Atlantic University

"Mark   visdom
that   e Jesus
of tl   assion
and   riends
wit   sisted
fan   ading
this
Mic

"In   elling
por   lfully
guic   such
as '   ' Student   read
and
Lynn

JESUS

BEHAVING

BADLY

THE PUZZLING PARADOXES
of the MAN *from* GALILEE

MARK L. STRAUSS

IVP Books

An imprint of InterVarsity Press
Downers Grove, Illinois

InterVarsity Press
P.O. Box 1400, Downers Grove, IL 60515-1426
ivpress.com
email@ivpress.com

InterVarsity Press® is the book-publishing division of InterVarsity Christian Fellowship/USA®, a
movement of students and faculty active on campus at hundreds of universities, colleges and schools
of nursing in the United States of America, and a member movement of the International Fellowship
of Evangelical Students. For information about local and regional activities, visit intervarsity.org.

All Scripture quotations, unless otherwise indicated, are taken from THE HOLY BIBLE, NEW
INTERNATIONAL VERSION®, NIV® Copyright © 1973, 1978, 1984, 2011 by Biblica, Inc.™ Used
by permission. All rights reserved worldwide.

Cover design: David Fassett
Interior design: Beth McGill

Images: Christ expelling the money changers from the temple: from the 'Small Passion' series,
pub 1511 by Duerer / Private Collection / Bridgeman Images.
>> Torn paper edge: © robynmac/iStockphoto
>> Overturned table: © LifesizeImages/iStockphoto

ISBN 978-0-8308-2466-3 (print)
ISBN 978-0-8308-9811-4 (digital)

Printed in the United States of America ∞

Library of Congress Cataloging-in-Publication Data

Strauss, Mark L., 1959-
  Jesus behaving badly : the puzzling paradoxes of the man from Galilee / Mark L. Strauss.
     pages cm
  Includes bibliographical references and index.
  ISBN 978-0-8308-2466-3 (pbk. : alk. paper)
  1. Jesus Christ--Person and offices. I. Title.
  BT203.S753 2015
  232--dc23

                                                                                    2015027565

| P | 20 | 19 | 18 | 17 | 16 | 15 | 14 | 13 | 12 | 11 | 10 | 9 | 8 | 7 | 6 | 5 | 4 | 3 | 2 | 1 |
| Y | 32 | 31 | 30 | 29 | 28 | 27 | 26 | 25 | 24 | 23 | 22 | 21 | 20 | 19 | 18 | 17 | 16 | 15 |

To Roxanne, Daniel, Jamie and Luke

Contents

Everybody Likes Jesus

*I am a Jew, but I am enthralled by the
luminous figure of the Nazarene.*

Albert Einstein

*I am a historian, I am not a believer, but I must confess
as a historian that this penniless preacher from Nazareth is
irrevocably the very center of history. Jesus Christ is
easily the most dominant figure in all history.*

H. G. Wells

*I like your Christ, I do not like your Christians.
Your Christians are so unlike your Christ.*

Mahatma Gandhi

The Doobie Brothers famously sang "Jesus is just alright with me,"[1] and that about sums it up. Just about everybody likes Jesus. Muslims like Jesus. They call him by his Arabic name, Isa, and view him as a great prophet, just a little behind Mohammad in power and authority. Jesus is particularly revered for his power to heal. It was later Christians, Muslims claim, who distorted the truth and falsely (and blasphemously) turned him into a deity—the Son of God.

Followers of the New Age love Jesus. They consider him to be one of the most enlightened people who ever lived, someone truly in touch with his divine self. By following his way, people can attain true enlightenment, their deity within. This is the yoga, tofu and wheat-grass Jesus.

Jews—at least those who study him historically—like Jesus. They view him as a reforming Jewish prophet who opposed the pride and hypocrisy of the ruling elite but tragically got himself crucified by the Roman authorities.

Even most atheists like Jesus. To many he was a good man and social reformer who preached that people should love one another and turn the other cheek. But the power-hungry church transformed this humble prophet into a divine miracle worker and Son of God, devising the far-fetched notion that his death paid the penalty for people's sins.

Yes, almost everyone likes Jesus—at least the particular version they choose to believe in. This is the kind and gentle Jesus. The Mr. Rogers lookalike who shows up on Sunday school flannelgraphs laughing and smiling with children on his lap and a twinkle in his eye. This is the "love your enemies" Jesus who always turns the other cheek. This is the good shepherd Jesus, striding confidently back to the flock with the little lost lamb contentedly draped across his shoulders.

Yet the New Testament itself paints a darker and more complex picture of Jesus. After all, how could the Mr. Rogers Jesus make more enemies than friends over the course of his life? How could he stir up the whole religious establishment to conclude that he was dangerous and must be eliminated? How could he have gotten himself arrested by the Roman authorities and executed in perhaps the most inhumane manner ever devised?

The record shows that Jesus said and did some things that appear puzzling at best and downright contemptible at worst. He told people to hate their families, to cut off body parts, and to eat his flesh and drink his blood.[2] He demanded perfection from his followers and warned that most people were straight on their way to hell (Mt 5:48; 7:13-14). He said that those who did not behave themselves would be cut up into little pieces (Mt 24:51//Lk 12:46).

Jesus called those who weren't Jewish "dogs" and upheld the special status of the Hebrews in a way we would call ethnocentric if not racist (Mk 7:24-30//Mt 15:21-28). With no women among the twelve apostles, he looks pretty chauvinistic. He apparently had anger issues, cursing a fig tree because it didn't have any fruit on it, and driving merchants out of the temple with a whip (Mk 11:12-24//Mt 21:12-22; Lk 19:45-47). He sent two thousands pigs to their death in the sea (Mk 5:1-20//Mt 8:28-34//Lk 8:26-39).

One person who didn't think Jesus was so great after all was English philosopher Bertrand Russell. In his famous essay "Why I Am Not a Christian," Russell claimed that Jesus was mistaken when he predicted that he would return within a generation, and unethical when he cursed a fig tree and caused the death of thousands of pigs. He found Jesus' teaching about hell particularly reprehensible: "There is one very serious defect to my mind in Christ's moral character, and that is that He believed in hell. I do not myself feel that any person who is really profoundly humane can believe in everlasting punishment."[3]

We tend to overlook Jesus' "bad behavior" and instead create a Jesus who is more palatable—one just like us. Albert Schweitzer pointed this out over a century ago in his classic volume *The Quest of the Historical Jesus*. Schweitzer wrote about the so-called first quest for the historical Jesus, when eighteenth- and nineteenth-century rationalistic scholars tried to find the "real" Jesus behind the supposedly naive and embellished accounts in the Gospels.

Schweitzer showed that these authors tended to ignore the context of first-century Judaism. They transformed Jesus from a wild-eyed apocalyptic prophet—the real Jesus according to Schweitzer—into a nineteenth-century gentleman and philanthropist. For them, Jesus was an inoffensive preacher proclaiming the fatherhood of God and brotherhood of man. In other words, Jesus became the mirror through which they saw themselves.

The same thing happens today. Soft-spoken Sunday school teachers tell stories in which Jesus appears a lot like Santa Claus, speaking kindly to the children and telling them to obey their parents. Punch and cookies await if they will listen and behave. At a men's conference Jesus is a man's man, with callused hands and burly muscles (a carpenter, after all!), who clears the temple like a linebacker. No one would mess with him today.

In a Chinese church, the picture of Jesus on the wall portrays him as Asian. In much of the Western world, he is white, with blond hair and blue eyes. Enter an African American church, and you might see a black Jesus.

Each year when I teach the Gospels, I open my first class by showing a variety of film clips from movies about Jesus. An amazing diversity of films have been produced over the years. From the somber, aloof and stilted Jesus of *The Greatest Story Ever Told* to the clown-faced folk singer of *Godspell*, to the conflicted, self-doubting and all-too-human Jesus of *The Last Temptation of Christ*, to the laughing, down-to-earth Jesus in *Jesus* (1999) who gets into a water fight with his disciples!

Why such diverse portraits of the man from Galilee? By almost any account Jesus is the most influential person in human history. About a third of the earth's population identifies as Christian— followers of Christ. Even our calendars identify his birth as the center point in human history. Everything before him is B.C., "before Christ." Everything after is A.D., *anno Domini*, "the year of the Lord." Though Jesus is the most talked about, written about, argued about and revered person on the planet, he is also the most enigmatic. Thousands of books have been written asking the question, who was this Jesus of Nazareth?

The question is simple but the answer obviously is not. One of the reasons for this is because the New Testament itself presents a complex and puzzling picture of Jesus. At times Jesus' words are difficult to understand, and scholars scratch their heads over them. What did Jesus mean when he told a man to "Let the dead bury their own dead" (Lk 9:60) or that "Everyone will be salted with fire" (Mk 9:49)? What is the "blasphemy against the Holy Spirit," and why is it a sin that cannot be forgiven (Mk 3:28-29// Mt 12:31-32)? What does it mean that "violent people" are taking the kingdom of God by force (Mt 11:12)? These are strange and puzzling sayings.

Other times the problem is not that Jesus' words are difficult to understand but that they are all too clear. As Mark Twain is reported to have quipped, "It's not those parts of the Bible that I can't understand that bother me; it's the parts that I do understand!"[4] Jesus said some very controversial things.

So who was Jesus? Was he a violent agitator who denounced the powerful elite and called on his followers to take up the sword? Or was he a pacifist calling people to love their enemies, turn the other cheek, go the extra mile and give without expecting anything in return? Was he a hellfire and damnation preacher telling people to repent or burn in hell? Or was he a gentle shepherd proclaiming God's unconditional love for all people? Was he profamily, encouraging people to stay married and love their children? Or did he tell people they should hate their parents, spouses and children, and join his new spiritual family (like some cults do today)? According to the New Testament Gospels, the answer to all these questions would seem to be yes!

We must resist the temptation to domesticate Jesus, to make him just like us. We have to remember that Jesus was not a twenty-first-century Christian. He lived in a world with major inequalities between men and women, between Romans and Jews, between slave and free. While he may have given indications of the direction these inequalities should go, he didn't seek immediate upheaval for any of them. Neither did he think or act like someone familiar with space travel, nuclear science, multinational corporations or video games. He came to a people and lived as a person who viewed the world very differently from how we view it today.

So when we observe Jesus' apparent bad behavior with reference to slaves or family values or the death of pigs or the cursing of fig trees, we are asked to view him as he is, not as we wish he were—not as someone with twenty-first-century sensibilities toward equality or the environment. We may not always be happy with the results, and we probably shouldn't expect to be. Ultimately we have to decide if we are going to sit in judgment on Jesus or listen and learn from him.

Jesus Behaving Badly looks at some of the puzzling and seemingly offensive things Jesus said and did, and tries to make sense of them. What we just might find is that when Jesus is at his most difficult, he is also at his most profound. When he surprises us, when we at first recoil at his words, deeper reflection brings even deeper truths. Some of the most important things we learn about Jesus and his mission—and about us—can be found in these enigmatic sayings and actions.

Revolutionary or Pacifist?

The King and His Kingdom

Gentle Jesus, meek and mild,
Look upon a little child;
Pity my simplicity,
Suffer me to come to Thee.

Charles Wesley,
"Gentle Jesus, Meek and Mild"

JAY LENO, FORMER HOST OF *The Tonight Show,* used to do a popular sketch called "Jaywalking," where he would interview people on the street. The bit could have been called "Are People Really That Dim?" since Leno would ask the most basic of questions and people would reveal their ignorance. For example, he once asked, "Who was the first man on the moon?" When someone answered (correctly!), "Armstrong," he asked, "And what was his first name?" The young lady replied, "Louie!" He asked another, "How many stars are on that flag?"—pointing to an American flag. The answer was, "I don't know; it's flapping too hard to count them."

When asked which countries border the United States, one guy responded, "Hmm . . . Australia . . . and Hawaii?" Pushing the limits of the not-so-bright-o-meter, Leno stumped another with, "Who wrote *The Autobiography of Malcolm X*?" (Knowing the high caliber of IVP book readers, I won't provide the answers.)

But here's one that shouldn't stump anyone: Who said, "Turn the other cheek" and "Blessed are the peacemakers"? My guess is that most people would remember that these are the words of Jesus. If there's one thing people know about Jesus, it's that he promoted a radical new ethic of love.

But other sayings of Jesus are not so well known, like, "I did not come to bring peace, but a sword" (Mt 10:34) or "I have come to bring fire on the earth!" (Lk 12:49). If Jay Leno asked people who made these statements, you might expect answers like Genghis Khan, Ivan the Terrible or Saddam Hussein. But not Jesus!

Many people think of Jesus as a pacifist, a cross between Mahatma Gandhi, Martin Luther King Jr. and Barney the Dinosaur. Yet he said some remarkably provocative things—things about swords, and fire and violent death. This is perhaps not surprising when we understand the first-century world in which he was born.

FIRST-CENTURY PALESTINE: REVOLUTION IN THE AIR

Some names aren't very popular today. There just aren't that many parents who name their daughters Jezebel. (Jezebel was the wicked queen of Israel who killed God's prophets and led Israel into idol worship.) There aren't many Adolfs or Neros. It's the same with Judas, which ranks very low in boys' names. After all, who wants to be named after the great archvillain of the Jesus story, the one who betrayed Jesus for thirty pieces of silver? A kid with that name is probably going to get beat up regularly in school.

But it wasn't always like that in Jewish history. Judas (or Judah or Jude—different forms of the same Hebrew name, Yehudah) was the name of the tribe of royalty among the twelve tribes of Israel and the one from which the Messiah was prophesied to come (Gen 49:9-10; Jer 23:5-6). It was the tribe of King David, Israel's greatest king, and of his son Solomon, whose riches and wisdom were world-renowned.

The name Judas gained even greater cachet during the period of the Maccabees in the second century B.C., when, after years of foreign rule, Judas Maccabeus led the Jews in revolt against the evil Syrian dictator Antiochus IV. Antiochus called himself *Epiphanes*, meaning "the divine one," but was nicknamed by his opponents *Epimanes*—"the madman"—because of his megalomania and erratic behavior. Antiochus sought to unite the Seleucid (Syrian) empire by eradicating the Jewish religion and forcibly converting the Jews to his own paganism. He desecrated the Jerusalem temple, offering sacrifices of pigs on the altar and ordering Jews not to circumcise their children. This was a crisis beyond belief, and Judaism teetered on the brink of annihilation.

Yet when a Syrian official came to the Jewish town of Modein to oversee a pagan sacrifice, a Jewish priest named Mattathias—Judas's father—stood up in resistance, refusing to offer the sacrifice. Enraged when another Jew stepped forward to make the sacrifice, Mattathias grabbed a spear and with one thrust ran it through both the Syrian official and his Jewish collaborator. Mattathias and his family fled into the hills and launched a guerrilla war against the Syrians. Now led by his son Judas—nicknamed Maccabeus, "the hammer," because of his prowess in battle—the Jewish rebels eventually took back Jerusalem and rededicated the temple. Jews today celebrate this victory in the feast of Hanukkah.

The Maccabean Revolt—with Judas as its hero—enshrined forever in Jewish history the noble cause of rising up to overthrow wicked oppressors. The Maccabees ruled for over a century (166–63 B.C.), until Judea again fell prey to a foreign adversary. This time it

was the voracious appetite of a growing power in the West—the
Roman Empire. When the Roman general Pompey arrived with his
legions in Palestine in 63 B.C., the Jewish state was divided by civil
war. Pompey quickly subjugated the weakened nation, and once
again the Jews found themselves under foreign rule. The Romans
placed a client king, Herod, on the throne, taxed the Jews heavily
and suppressed with violent force any hint of revolt.

Some Jews welcomed the stability of the *Pax Romana*, the "Roman
peace." Others accepted it grudgingly as God's judgment for Israel's
unfaithfulness. Still others mobilized against the oppressors, striking
back against the Romans and their Jewish collaborators. The Sicarii,
or "dagger men," were one such group. With razor-sharp daggers
hidden in their cloaks, they would mingle with the crowds at festivals,
stabbing their victims and then disappearing into the throng.[1]

Sporadically throughout the first century, revolts broke out, challenging Roman hegemony. Each time the Roman legions moved in
and ruthlessly crushed the revolt. One such revolt occurred in A.D.
6, when another Judas—"Judas of Galilee"—led a tax revolt against
the Romans. Judas mocked his countrymen as cowards for paying
taxes out of fear to their human overlords rather than trusting in
God, their true Lord and King.[2] Judas's fate is unknown, though his
two sons, James and Simon, were later arrested and crucified under
the Roman governor Tiberius Julius Alexander.[3]

Other revolutionary actions followed throughout the first
century. There was Theudas, a self-proclaimed prophet (the Jewish
historian Josephus calls him an "imposter"), who in about A.D.
44–46 gathered many followers and claimed that at his command
the Jordan River would part and his people would walk through on
dry land (see Josh 3). In the end the only thing that parted was
Theudas's head from his body, as the Roman governor Fadus sent a
contingent of Roman cavalry who massacred many of the rebels
and seized Theudas alive. Beheading him, they carried his head

back to Jerusalem—a gruesome warning to the population of the fate that awaited all those who challenged the might of Rome.[4]

Then there was an Egyptian prophet who, during the governorship of Felix (A.D. 52–58), led four thousand assassins (Sicarii?) into the wilderness (Acts 21:38). Josephus tells about this same Egyptian, calling him a "false prophet" and saying he had thirty thousand followers. He claimed that at his command the walls of Jerusalem would fall, just like those of mighty Jericho (see Josh 6). Needless to say, the walls stayed in place, as did the Roman troops who were sent to quell the rebellion. What fell were the people's hopes for redemption. Though the Egyptian escaped and was never heard from again, the Romans killed hundreds of his followers and scattered the rest.[5]

As these would-be saviors came and went, the disillusioned Jewish people of Jesus' day longed for the day when God would raise up their *true* king, the Messiah from David's line, the one predicted by the prophets. They remembered Isaiah's great prophecy:

> For to us a child is born,
> > to us a son is given,
> > and the government will be on his shoulders. . . .
> He will reign on David's throne
> > and over his kingdom,
> establishing and upholding it
> > with justice and righteousness
> > from that time on and forever. (Is 9:6-7)

This great king would crush Israel's enemies and establish a just and righteous kingdom:

> With righteousness he will judge the needy,
> > with justice he will give decisions for the poor of the
> > > earth.

He will strike the earth with the rod of his mouth;
    with the breath of his lips he will slay the wicked. (Is 11:4)

Into this climate Jesus was born: at a time when peasant farmers in the Galilee eked out a living and muttered under their breath about oppressive Roman taxes and cruel Gentile overlords, and when frustrated young men would head into the hills to meet up with roving bands of rebels, hoping to be heroes in the great war of liberation.

Did Jesus, like so many of his people, hope and expect God to raise up a savior who would overthrow the Romans and establish God's kingdom on earth? Did he himself have messianic ambitions, thinking he might be the One?

WAS JESUS A REVOLUTIONARY?

In 1967 S. G. F. Brandon wrote a book called *Jesus and the Zealots*, in which he argued that Jesus was an insurrectionist who was executed for rebellion against the Roman Empire. This thesis has been revived recently by Reza Aslan in his 2013 *New York Times* bestseller, *Zealot*. Aslan claims that though Jesus was not necessarily a violent revolutionary himself, he followed the zealot doctrine, a nationalistic perspective that God alone is the sovereign of Israel and that the Romans were illegitimate rulers. This zealot perspective, and more particularly Jesus' actions in the temple, got Jesus crucified as an insurrectionist.

Aslan reaches his conclusions about Jesus through a highly selective reading of texts. He ignores large swaths of the Jesus tradition, including sayings and actions considered authentic even by the most liberal of New Testament scholars. He builds his case on the general revolutionary milieu of first-century Palestine, rather than on the actual historical evidence about Jesus of Nazareth. Yet, while his methodology is flawed, his fundamental question is legitimate: Was Jesus a political revolutionary? Some of the evidence certainly points in this direction:

1. It is universally recognized that Jesus' primary message concerned the kingdom of God and its imminent arrival. When Jesus began his public ministry he announced, "The kingdom of God has come near" (Mk 1:15). What would the phrase *kingdom of God* have meant to a first-century Jew? While most Christians today think of God's kingdom as something spiritual and internal, Jesus' Jewish contemporaries would envision something closer to the guy on the street corner with a sign reading "The End of the World Is Here!" It would certainly mean that God is king and Caesar is not, and so Roman authority over Jerusalem and the temple is illegitimate. Was Jesus announcing that God would soon overthrow the Roman Empire?

2. One of Jesus' disciples, Simon, was a "Zealot" (Mt 10:4//Mk 3:18//Lk 6:15; Acts 1:13), which could indicate revolutionary sympathies among Jesus' followers.[6]

3. Jesus affirmed the message of John the Baptist, who predicted a coming fiery judgment. John's announcement that "the ax is already at the root of the trees" and that "every tree that does not produce good fruit will be cut down and thrown into the fire" (Lk 3:9//Mt 3:10) indicates a soon-to-come violent upheaval of society. John also spoke of the "coming One" (the Messiah) who would use his winnowing fork to gather his wheat to the barn (for protection) but would "burn up the chaff with unquenchable fire" (Lk 3:17//Mt 3:12). This seems to be a vision of violent judgment enacted by the warrior Messiah.

4. Jesus seemed to have affirmed this role for himself when he said, "I have come to bring fire on the earth, and how I wish it were already kindled!" (Lk 12:49).

5. Jesus said on one occasion that he did not come to bring peace but a sword, and to turn

a man against his father,
  a daughter against her mother,
a daughter-in-law against her mother-in-law.
    (Mt 10:34-35//Lk 12:51-53)

This sounds like a provocation to violent opposition. Furthermore, as his enemies closed in on him, Jesus encouraged his followers to sell their cloaks and buy a sword (Lk 22:36-38).

6. There is little doubt that Jesus' followers believed he was "the Christ." The name "Jesus the Christ" or "Jesus Christ" appears in our earliest Christian writings (e.g., 1 Thess 1:1, 3; Gal 1:1, 3; Jas 1:1; 2:1). "Christ" (Greek: *christos*) is the Greek translation of the Hebrew *mashiach*, "Messiah," meaning the "anointed one." Originally used as a title for Israel's king ("the Lord's Anointed"), it was coming into use in the first century with reference to Israel's end-time savior, who would establish God's kingdom.

Scholars debate whether the title Messiah/Christ was first applied to Jesus before or after his resurrection, but there is no doubt that his earliest followers identified him as such. Though there was a variety of views about the nature and identity of the Messiah in first-century Judaism, the most pervasive and dominant expectation concerned a coming king from David's line who would crush Israel's enemies, judge its unrighteous rulers, and establish God's rule of justice and peace. A Jewish collection of psalms, written shortly before the time of Jesus, expresses this hope for the coming "son of David" (the Messiah):

See, Lord, and raise up for them their king,
    the son of David, to rule over your servant Israel
    in the time known to you, O God.
Undergird him with the strength to destroy the unrighteous
        rulers;
    to purge Jerusalem from gentiles

> who trample her to destruction;
> in wisdom and in righteousness to drive out
> the sinners from the inheritance;
> to smash the arrogance of sinners
> like a potter's jar;
> To shatter all their substance with an iron rod;
> to destroy the unlawful nations with the word of his mouth.
> (Psalms of Solomon 17:21-25)[7]

The question then becomes, Why did Jesus' followers choose this title to describe him? He must have said or done things that convinced them he was this coming king.

7. It is almost universally acknowledged that Jesus conducted some kind of subversive action in the temple at Passover time, and that this action provoked his crucifixion (Mt 21:12-16//Mk 11:15-18// Lk 19:45-47; cf. Jn 2:14-25). Such a challenge to the authority of the temple leadership would have been identified as both blasphemy and sedition, an attack on the religious and political leadership.

8. Jesus was crucified by the Romans as "king of the Jews." All four Gospels say that a placard was placed above Jesus on the cross identifying him by this mocking title (Mt 27:37//Mk 15:26//Lk 23:38// Jn 19:19). Most scholars consider this to be a historically reliable tradition, since we know from other sources that crucifixion victims often had a declaration of their crimes publicly displayed. Furthermore, this piece of tradition is unlikely to have been invented by the early Christians, since the title "King" was not widely used in their worship (Lord, Messiah, Son of God, were the titles of choice). Jesus is then repeatedly mocked on the cross as "Messiah" and "king of the Jews," further evidence that this was the charge made against him.

9. Finally, Jesus was crucified together with insurrectionists, suggesting his crimes were considered the same as theirs. The two men crucified beside Jesus are identified as "robbers" (*lēstai*) by

Matthew and Mark (Mt 27:38//Mk 15:27 ESV) and "criminals" (*kakourgoi*) by Luke (Lk 23:32). These were probably not thieves, per se, but insurrectionists. The Romans used these kinds of terms to describe rebels, identifying them not as revolutionaries (which sounds noble) but as common criminals. It is much the same today. Those who support a revolutionary movement will call its rebels "freedom fighters." Those who oppose it will refer to them as "terrorists," "thugs" or "criminals." These two victims were likely companions of Barabbas, who is identified as a notorious prisoner arrested for taking part in insurrection and murder (Mt 27:16//Mk 15:7//Lk 23:19). Jesus is crucified as "king of the Jews"—a royal pretender—beside two (other?) insurrectionists.

So, was Jesus a revolutionary, encouraging his followers to take violent action against the Romans? Despite these passages and arguments, there is overwhelming evidence that Jesus opposed violence and retribution.

BLESSED ARE THE PEACEMAKERS

Some of Jesus' most unique and undisputed teaching concerns loving enemies, refusing to retaliate and repaying evil with good. In Jesus' Sermon on the Mount, his inaugural kingdom address, he says, "Blessed are the peacemakers, for they will be called children of God" (Mt 5:9). In a time where violent retribution was all too common, he encouraged his hearers not to lash back but to turn the other cheek (Mt 5:39//Lk 6:29). If someone sues you and takes your tunic—the shirt off your back—you should bless them by giving them your coat as well (Mt 5:40). This was to be true even against the hated Romans. If conscripted to carry a soldier's bag for one mile, Jesus said to carry it a second mile (Mt 5:41).

This was radical teaching. Conventional wisdom said to love your friends and hate your enemies. Jesus refers to this traditional perspective in Matthew 5:43: "You have heard that it was said, 'Love your neighbor and hate your enemy.'" The first part of this command comes from the Old Testament: "Love your neighbor" (Lev 19:18). The second part about hating enemies is not in the Bible, but was common folk wisdom in Jesus' day. A popular Jewish book of wisdom, *The Wisdom of Jesus ben Sirach*, written a little before the time of Jesus, puts it this way:

> Give to the devout, but do not help the sinner.
> Do good to the humble, but do not give to the ungodly;
> hold back their bread, and do not give it to them,
> for by means of it they might subdue you;
> then you will receive twice as much evil
> for all the good you have done to them.
> For the Most High also hates sinners
> and will inflict punishment on the ungodly.
> Give to the one who is good, but do not help the sinner.
> (Sirach 12:4-7 NRSV)

The first-century Jewish group known as the Essenes, who produced the Dead Sea Scrolls, had a similar perspective. They withdrew from society, viewing the Jewish leadership in Jerusalem as corrupt. The Dead Sea Scroll called the *Rule of the Community* (1QS) encourages the members of the community to "love the sons of light . . . and hate all the sons of darkness."[8] The "sons of light" are their own people, while the "sons of darkness" are the Jerusalem priesthood, the Romans and their supporters. It was common sense to love your friends and to hate your enemies. That's why we call them enemies!

Jesus, however, radically challenged this. He called on his followers to "love your enemies and pray for those who persecute you" (Mt 5:44). This is widely recognized by scholars of every stripe as one of Jesus' most distinctive teachings. It is the essence of who he was and what he came to do. It was also the inspiration for great

advocates of nonviolent resistance in the service of civil rights, like
Mahatma Gandhi and Martin Luther King Jr.[9]

Jesus also went so far as to affirm the legitimacy of Caesar's rule.
When his enemies tried to trap him by asking him whether it was
right for them to pay taxes to Caesar, Jesus famously replied, "Give
back to Caesar what is Caesar's and to God what is God's" (Mk
12:17//Mt 22:21//Lk 20:25). The question of course was a trap. The
religious leaders knew that if Jesus affirmed the legitimacy of taxes
to Rome, the common people, who hated Roman oppression and
taxation, would despise him. On the other hand, if he opposed
Roman taxation he could be accused of insurrection and rebellion.

Jesus' brilliant response affirmed Caesar's authority over a particular sphere, but not over the things of God. Of course the bril-
liance of his response is partly in its ambiguity. Since all authority
is ultimately God's, to give Caesar what is his could mean to give
him nothing, since everything belongs to God! Whether or not this
was part of Jesus' intention, his answer was certainly not that of a
violent revolutionary who would have rejected altogether the authority of Caesar.

REVOLUTIONARY OR PACIFIST? JESUS' MISSION AND THE KINGDOM OF GOD

So was Jesus a violent agitator or a pacifist? Did he come to bring a
sword or an olive branch? The answer to this paradox takes us to the
heart of Jesus' mission, purpose and vision of the kingdom of God.

What sort of king? As we have seen, there is little doubt that
Jesus was executed as a king, a pretender to the throne. He was
crucified with insurrectionists and with a placard calling him "king
of the Jews" above his head. His followers called him "the anointed
one"—*Mashiach* and *Christos*—the promised end-time king from
David's line. But what kind of Messiah did Jesus claim to be? And
what did he hope to accomplish?

The clearest answer to this question came when Jesus took his disciples away from their bustling ministry in Galilee for a spiritual retreat. They headed north of the Sea of Galilee to the lush, well-watered region of Caesarea Philippi, near the headwaters of the Jordan River. On the way he asked them a question, "Who do people say I am?" They responded by noting the popular speculations about Jesus: "Some say John the Baptist; others say Elijah; and still others, one of the prophets." Jesus pressed them, "But what about you? . . . Who do you say I am?" Peter, so often the spokesman, answered for the rest, "You are the Messiah" (Mk 8:27-29; cf. Mt 16:13-16//Lk 9:18-20). Peter had been hearing Jesus' authoritative teaching and seeing his amazing miracles. He finally came to the (correct!) conclusion that Jesus was the Messiah, the promised King and Savior of Israel.

Jesus' response, however, was shocking. He did not deny that he was the Messiah but instead ordered the disciples not to tell anyone (Mk 8:30). This is part of the so-called messianic secret, one of the most puzzling features in the Gospels. Jesus repeatedly silences demons, tells those who are healed not to tell others and tells his disciples to keep his identity a secret. The reason for these commands has been the source of endless speculation among scholars, but is almost certainly related to Jesus' determination to *define his messiahship on his own terms*. And that is precisely what he does here: "He then began to teach them that the Son of Man must suffer many things and be rejected by the elders, the chief priests and the teachers of the law, and that he must be killed and after three days rise again" (Mk 8:31; cf. Mt 16:21//Lk 9:22).

When Peter correctly identifies Jesus as the Messiah, Jesus defines this messiahship not as the traditional warrior king from David's line who would crush Israel's enemies and establish God's reign in Jerusalem. Instead, he draws from the much more obscure Jewish taproot—the Suffering Servant of the Lord of Isaiah 53:

He was pierced for our transgressions,
   he was crushed for our iniquities;
the punishment that brought us peace was on him,
   and by his wounds we are healed. (Is 53:5)

The Messiah, Jesus says, will be rejected by Israel's leaders and will be killed. This shocking statement is too much for Peter, and he does what any self-respecting Jewish patriot would do. He calls out Jesus for such a defeatist attitude, rebuking him. Jesus responds by rebuking Peter right back, with even stronger words: "Get behind me, Satan! . . . You do not have in mind the concerns of God, but merely human concerns" (Mk 8:32-33).

In what sense were Peter's words satanic? Here we might recall Jesus' temptation in the wilderness at the beginning of his ministry (Mt 4:1-11//Lk 4:1-11; cf. Mk 1:12-13). Jesus is tested by Satan in three areas: turning stones into bread to alleviate his hunger, jumping from the pinnacle of the temple to test God's divine protection, and worshiping Satan to receive authority over the kingdoms of the world. Each of these is a challenge for Jesus to take the easy path as the Messiah—achieve what he desires without trusting in God or following God's way.

God's plan is to provide Jesus with sustenance (bread), but he will do it only after Jesus has experienced severe hunger. God's plan is to provide divine protection and deliverance, but he will do it only after Jesus has willingly given up his life for others. God's plan is to give Jesus the kingdoms of the world as his inheritance. But he will do so only after Jesus has achieved his throne through his death, resurrection and ascension to the right hand of God. The path to glory will go through suffering. The Davidic warrior king must first sacrifice himself for his people.

What sort of kingdom? The battle is engaged. If Jesus defined his role as the Messiah as a suffering one, what did he hope to accomplish? What kind of kingdom was he here to establish? Key clues come from the authoritative actions of Jesus. We tend to think of Jesus' miracles as acts of compassion or perhaps as evidence of his divine authority. They are certainly this. But they are much more. Jesus' miracles are symbolic actions meant to teach lessons about the nature of the kingdom and the purpose for which he came. There are four main types of miracles in the Gospels: healings, exorcisms, resurrections (or revivifications) and nature miracles. Each carries symbolic significance.

A key clue concerning the significance of Jesus' healings comes in a question posed by John the Baptist. By all accounts John was a strange bird. He dressed in animal skins with a leather belt around his waist, recalling Elijah and the prophets of old. He withdrew to the desert like a hermit, living off the land by eating locusts and honey (I prefer my locusts with ketchup). His message was a warning of a fiery judgment that was coming to consume the enemies of God. The agent of this judgment would be God's Messiah—"the coming One."

John might have been dismissed as a harmless eccentric, except for the fact that many people were following him. Herod Antipas, son of Herod the Great and tetrarch of Galilee and Perea, became concerned. According to Josephus this concern resulted from John's growing popularity.[10] The Gospels cite a more specific reason: John had denounced Herod's affair with his brother's wife, Herodias, whom he had married after divorcing his first wife. Herod had John arrested and thrown in prison (Mt 14:3-5//Mk 6:17-20).

It was there that John began to have doubts about Jesus. Earlier he had been convinced that Jesus was indeed the coming One, the Messiah, the agent of God's salvation. Now he wasn't quite sure. Jesus was not doing the things John expected of the Messiah. Shouldn't he be raising an army and preparing for war? When would he start "baptizing" the enemies of God with the fire of judgment (Lk 3:16)? Because of these rising doubts, John sent some of his disciples to ask Jesus, "Are you the one who is to come, or should we expect someone else?" (Lk 7:18-23//Mt 11:2-6).

Jesus responds by telling them to report back to John what they had seen and heard: "The blind receive sight, the lame walk, those who have leprosy are cleansed, the deaf hear, the dead are raised, and the good news is proclaimed to the poor" (Lk 7:22//Mt 11:5).

Jesus points to his miracles of healing and his announcement of good news as confirmation that he is indeed the coming One—the Messiah. It is important to note that Jesus is not saying, "Look at my miraculous power; I must be the Messiah!" Nor is he saying, "See what compassion I have; I must be the One." He is instead alluding to Isaiah 35:5-6 and other key passages in Isaiah that describe God's final salvation, when he will restore creation to its perfect state (cf. Is 26:19; 29:18-21; 61:1). Isaiah 35, after referring to the eyes of the blind seeing again, the deaf hearing, the lame walking and the mute shouting, continues:

> Water will gush forth in the wilderness
> and streams in the desert. . . .
> No lion will be there,
> nor any ravenous beast; . . .
> But only the redeemed will walk there,
> and those the LORD has rescued will return.
> They will enter Zion with singing;
> everlasting joy will crown their heads.
> Gladness and joy will overtake them,
> and sorrow and sighing will flee away. (Is 35:6, 9-10)

The desert restored, violence removed, eternal joy and the end of sorrow. This text is thoroughly eschatological, that is, describing God's end-time salvation, when he will remove the curse from the earth and restore the perfection of Eden. We learn here that Jesus' miracles are much more than evidence of his messianic identity. They are "previews of coming attractions," like movie trailers for the next blockbuster about to be released. They advertise the end of this present evil age and beginning of the age to come. They are evidence that God's end-time salvation is arriving through Jesus' words and actions. This is the kingdom of God.

The kingdom as restoration of creation. The same restoration of creation motif is associated with Jesus' other miracles— resuscitations, exorcisms and nature miracles. Three times in the Gospels Jesus restores life to someone who has died: a widow's son in Nain (Lk 7:11-16), Jairus's daughter (Mk 5:21-43//Mt 9:18-26//Lk 8:40-56) and Lazarus (Jn 11). It has often been noted that these are not true resurrections to glorified, immortal existence (1 Cor 15:52-53), since in each case Jesus restores a dead person to normal mortal life. They are resuscitations or revivifications. Jesus will be the first to rise from the dead in a glorified, imperishable body. He is the "firstborn from among the dead" (Col 1:18; cf. Rom 8:29) and the "firstfruits" of those who have died (1 Cor 15:20, 23). The resuscitations in the Gospels are therefore previews or snapshots of the coming defeat of death and the final resurrection (see Dan 12:2-3). As Jesus tells Martha before raising Lazarus, "I am the resurrection and the life" (Jn 11:25). His life resurrection will bring about the death of death itself (1 Cor 15:50-57).

The exorcisms too are evidence of God's restoration of a fallen creation. They indicate that Satan's forces are being defeated and that the kingdom of God is triumphing over the kingdom of Satan. When Jesus sends out seventy of his disciples to heal and to cast out demons, they return saying, "Lord, even the demons submit to us in your name." Jesus responds, "I saw Satan fall like lightning from heaven" (Lk 10:17-18). The exorcisms symbolize the defeat of Satan and his expulsion from heaven.

When Jesus is accused by the religious leaders of casting out demons by Satan's power, he first refutes the notion that Satan would cast out his own forces, and then adds, "If I drive out demons by the finger of God, *then the kingdom of God has come upon you*" (Lk 11:20//Mt 12:28). This is war!—the kingdom of God versus the kingdom of Satan. Jesus is claiming back captured territory and captured people. In a short parable Jesus identifies himself as a "stronger man" who is entering and plundering the house of a "strong man" (Satan) (Lk 11:21-22//Mt 12:29). Exorcisms are evidence that Jesus is entering and defeating Satan's realm, taking back those enslaved by him.

Nature miracles, too, carry eschatological significance. Nature miracles include things like walking on water, calming the storm, feeding the multitudes with a few loaves and fish, and turning water to wine. These function as acted-out parables, demonstrating Jesus' authority over a fallen creation and his ability to bring restoration and healing.

Notice what we see here about these four categories of miracles:

- Healings: *restoring fallen humanity*

- Nature miracles: *restoring fallen creation*

- Exorcisms: *defeating Satan*

- Resuscitations: *defeating death itself*

What do all these have in common? They do not take us back to the glory days of the kingdom of David or the period of Israel's independence under the Maccabees. All four go back much further—to the Garden of Eden. When Adam and Eve ate the forbidden fruit and Satan gained the upper hand, they fell from grace and became fallen creatures. There sin entered the world and death through sin. There creation itself was placed under a curse. Jesus' miracles confirm that he is not here to defeat the Roman legions or re-establish Israel's glorious empire. He has a much greater goal. He is here to defeat humanity's ultimate foes: disease, death, sin and Satan. He is here to reverse the results of the fall and to bring restoration to a fallen world.

CONCLUSION

So was Jesus a violent agitator? Was he a revolutionary? Did he come to bring a sword? Did he come to bring fire upon the earth? Absolutely! All of the above. But the revolution he inaugurated was not against the Roman legions. It was against the true enemies of humanity, the forces that have enslaved people from the beginning. It was a revolution against Satan and his demonic forces, taking back people who have fallen prey to their power. It was against sin that separated them from their God and alienated them from one another. It was against disease and death that destroyed the good life he had created. True victory over these forces came not through violent reprisal against those who perpetuated evil, but through the self-sacrificial death of God's Son. This is the paradox of the cross. Through his atoning death on the cross, Jesus conquered Satan, sin and death.

This is why Jesus calls his disciples to be peacemakers, to give instead of take, to love instead of hate, to go the extra mile, to live a life of self-sacrifice. By giving himself as a sacrifice for the sins, Jesus defeated his enemies and brought reconciliation between God and humanity. The people of God are called to emulate their Savior and conquer evil in the same way, not by perpetrating evil for evil but by overcoming evil with good.

"This is how we know what love is: Jesus Christ laid down his life for us. And we ought to lay down our lives for our brothers and sisters" (1 Jn 3:16).

Angry or Loving?

Prophet of Israel's Restoration

I **GREW UP IN A HOME OF FOUR BOYS:** three brothers (and no sisters). We were intensely competitive. Whether it was playing football, wrestling in the family room or playing a board game, all of us wanted to win. We hated to lose. Perhaps the worst game ever invented for a household like mine was the board game *Risk*. The goal of *Risk* is simple enough: to conquer the world. Everyone begins with a set number of countries and armies. You then attack and conquer other countries by rolling dice and defeating armies, until one person eventually conquers it all. It's a great game for aspiring dictators and megalomaniacs.

I remember one game in particular. I started in a relatively weak position (holding much of Europe—a position vulnerable to attack on all sides). But then two of my brothers went after each other, decimating each other's armies and leaving both of them vulnerable. I seized the opportunity and struck hard. I gained country after country, continent after continent. Visions of world domination danced in my head. I was going to win! But as suddenly as my hopes were raised, they were dashed, as the dice gods turned against me. Time and time again I lost the roll and my (clearly superior) troops were inexplicably vanquished. It was not fair! My once-strong position turned into weakness. My armies were decimated and my land swallowed up. I was the first player eliminated. (I hate this game.)

That was the problem with *Risk*. It raised expectations and then dashed them to pieces. We had a rule with games like this in our house: "Winner cleans up." It always worked well because by the end of the game, the loser was angry and sullen and depressed, and would shove the board on the floor, scattering the pieces. The winner was so excited and jubilant he didn't care and would happily clean up. It was a perfect symbiotic relationship: angry and destructive versus happy and restorative.

Risk taught us that we live in a dog-eat-dog world. The goal is to crush and humiliate your opponents. The game capitalizes on our fallen human nature. It feeds on our desire to dominate others and to win at all costs. The game frustrates so because it raises hopes and then dashes them to the ground. That seems to be the pattern with most conflicts in life. We have hopes and expectations about ourselves and others. When others throw cold water on these dreams or don't live up to our expectations, we get angry and defensive.

I wonder how Jesus would do playing *Risk*. We think of Jesus as a deeply spiritual, humble and self-sacrificial person. He spent whole nights in prayer. He taught that people should love their enemies and should forgive others not just once or twice or seven times, but seven times seventy times! He showed compassion for the multitudes, teaching them and feeding them miraculously with loaves and fish. He raised back to life the only son of a poor widow and the only daughter of a synagogue leader. He wept bitterly when his friend Lazarus died and then restored him to life and to his sisters. Ultimately and most importantly, he went to the cross and sacrificed himself for the world he loved.

Yet Jesus did not always play well with others. On some occasions he seems angry, vindictive and even mean-spirited. He gets angry at a fig tree for not producing fruit and curses it (even though it wasn't the season for figs). He goes into a fit of rage in the temple in Jerusalem, driving out the sellers of sacrificial animals and money-changers (this despite the fact that these merchants played an essential role in the daily function of the temple). He repeatedly humiliates his opponents and calls them names like "children of Satan" and "brood of vipers" (i.e., "your momma was a snake!"). How can the one who washed the feet of his disciples in humble service and told people to love even their enemies seem at times so angry and vindictive? Did Jesus have anger issues?

JESUS' CONFLICTS WITH THE RELIGIOUS LEADERS

As we read the Gospels, it is clear that conflict was a major aspect of Jesus' ministry. Surprisingly, these conflicts were not primarily with "bad" people. In fact he seems to have gotten along quite well with the lower classes of society—the poor, peasants, sinners, tax collectors, prostitutes and other riffraff. He spent so much time with them that his opponents even accused him of being "a glutton and a drunkard, a friend of tax collectors and sinners" (Mt 11:19//Lk 7:34). His primary conflicts were instead with the religious establishment, the "good" people. The issue was primarily one of turf. Jesus, an upstart rabbi, was viewed as a threat to their power and influence.

Growing popularity. One of the central themes of the Gospels is Jesus' growing popularity. He was clearly a charismatic personality whose teaching mesmerized the crowds. As Mark says, "The people were amazed at his teaching, because he taught them as one who had authority, not as the teachers of the law" (Mk 1:22; cf. Mt 7:28//Lk 4:32). While the scribes—the experts in religious law—repeated verbatim the traditions of the rabbis before them ("Rabbi so-and-so said . . ."), Jesus spoke with freshness and originality. He used an enormous range of teaching tools: parables, proverbs, metaphors, hyperbole, riddles, puns.

Jesus could have simply said, "It is impossible for a rich person, while trusting in their riches, to enter the kingdom of God." But instead he said, "It is easier for a camel to go through the eye of a needle than for someone who is rich to enter the kingdom of God" (Mk 10:25; cf. Mt 19:24//Lk 18:25). Who can forget this absurdly provocative image: a ginormous camel trying to squeeze itself through a tiny eye of a needle? That would make a wonderful *Far Side* cartoon. I can see it now: the camel would have squeezed only one small nose hair through the needle's eye, and the caption would read, "Almost there!"

Or what about Jesus' word picture for hypocrisy: a man with a giant plank in his eye trying to remove a speck from the eye of his friend (Mt 7:3-5//Lk 6:41-42)? I can imagine this one as a skit on the classic *Carol Burnett Show* (you'll have to go back to TV Land archives if you don't know this one). The scene would be in a doctor's office with Harvey Korman as the patient with a tiny speck in his eye. The doctor, Tim Conway, would enter the office with a beam protruding from his face. He would wreak havoc with every turn, knocking down filing cabinets, chairs and nurses.

Jesus was a master storyteller, and his parables were among his most memorable teaching tools. Everyone loves a good story, especially one with a twist at the end. And Jesus' parables often have a surprising twist. I tell my students that Jesus' parables are like mousetraps. They lure you in with a big piece of cheese (or peanut butter—more effective in my experience). They are stories from everyday life that people can relate to. You begin to identify with certain characters in the story. You know where this one is going. And then, *snap!* The trap catches you in some surprising way, pointing out an area of spiritual failure.

Consider the parable of the Pharisee and the tax collector (Lk 18:9-14). Two men go into the temple to pray, one a respected and revered Pharisee, the other a hated tax collector. Tax collectors

were despised because of their collusion with the Roman oppressors and because they were notorious cheats. From the perspective of Jesus' hearers, the outcome is already clear: God will
bless the pious Pharisee and curse the evil, traitorous tax collector.
Yet when the Pharisee prays a prayer of self-congratulation and the
tax collector one of humble contrition, Jesus shockingly announces
that only the tax collector left the temple right with God, "For all
those who exalt themselves will be humbled, and those who humble
themselves will be exalted" (Lk 18:14). The hearers would have been
shocked, but also impressed, by this surprising twist.

Indicting Israel's leaders. Many of the surprising twists in Jesus'
parables are at the expense of the religious leaders. Consider the
parable of the good Samaritan, where a despised Samaritan shows
compassion to a wounded man, while two of Israel's religious leaders
pass by on the other side of the road (Lk 10:25-37). Or the parable of
the great banquet (Lk 14:16-24; cf. Mt 22:2-14), where the original
invited guests (representing Israel's religious elite) make excuses and
so miss out on God's great salvation banquet, while lower-class outsiders feast at the master's table. Jesus turns to the privileged upper
class and says, "Guess who's *not* coming to dinner—you!"

Of course it is not just Jesus' teaching that delighted the crowds
and increased his popularity; it was also his miracles. One of the
most undisputed facts about Jesus was that he was renowned as
a healer and exorcist. And like his teaching, this attracted the
crowds by the thousands. People would travel great distances in
hopes of experiencing his healing power. A typical statement is
found in Mark 1:33-34, where Jesus is in a house in Capernaum:
"The whole town gathered at the door, and Jesus healed many who
had various diseases. He also drove out many demons."[1] The
crowds push forward in hope of touching Jesus' robe to be healed
(Mk 3:10; Lk 6:19; Mt 9:21//Mk 5:28). Wherever Jesus went, people
followed for healing:

When they had crossed over, they landed at Gennesaret and anchored there. As soon as they got out of the boat, people recognized Jesus. They ran throughout that whole region and carried the sick on mats to wherever they heard he was. And wherever he went—into villages, towns or countryside—they placed the sick in the marketplaces. They begged him to let them touch even the edge of his cloak, and all who touched it were healed. (Mk 6:53-56//Mt 14:34-36)

Not just Jesus' engaging teaching and marvelous miracles attracted the crowds, but also the content of his teaching. He made it clear that he was on their side. He announced blessings on the poor, the hungry and the oppressed (Lk 6:20). He promised a coming great reversal of fortunes, when the rich and mighty would be brought low, and the poor and humble would be exalted. This was certainly good news for the poor peasants of Galilee, but not so good for the ruling elite.

Jesus' announcement of the kingdom of God was also highly provocative. It would have seemed so not only to the political leaders of Palestine but also to the scribes and Pharisees, who viewed themselves as Israel's spiritual caretakers. If Jesus claimed to be inaugurating *God's* kingdom, then what were they caretakers of? What was Jesus bringing that they did not already have? By claiming to be God's instrument to establish his kingdom, Jesus was calling the present leadership illegitimate, saying they were frauds.

The same can be said for Jesus' selection of *twelve* special disciples. These twelve were no doubt meant to symbolize the restoration of the twelve tribes of Israel, and so the *true Israel*. At one point Jesus said that when he, the Son of Man, assumed his glorious throne, these twelve would sit on twelve thrones, judging the twelve tribes of Israel (Mt 19:28//Lk 22:30). How impudent for this young rabbi to claim that his ragtag band of followers would be the rulers of Israel's glorious kingdom!

All of these things—engaging teaching, astonishing miracles, claims to authority over Israel—drew people *to* Jesus, and subsequently *away from the other religious leaders*. It is not surprising that they viewed him as a threat, and a dangerous one at that.

Jesus on the offensive (or just being offensive?). Jesus wasn't doing much to build bridges of peace and harmony. He never seemed in the mood to sit around the campfire and sing "Kumbaya" with these guys. In fact, he seems to have taken every opportunity to tick them off. Time and time again in the Gospels Jesus is involved in conflict with the religious leaders. They accused him of blasphemy when he claimed authority to forgive sins (Mk 2:7//Mt 9:3//Lk 5:21). When he healed a man on the Sabbath, they accused him of breaking the law of Moses and plotted his death (Mk 3:6//Mt 12:14//Lk 6:11). When he cast out demons, they accused him of being possessed by Beelzebul (a name for Satan) and casting out demons by Satan's power (Mk 3:22//Mt 12:24//Lk 11:15; Mt 9:34).

Since Jesus taught his followers to "turn the other cheek" (Mt 5:39//Lk 6:29), we might expect him to do the same. But instead Jesus fires back. Twelve times in Matthew's Gospel alone he calls the religious leaders "hypocrites." Jesus' strongest response occurs in Matthew 23. Jesus tells his hearers to listen to the teaching of the Pharisees, but not to do what they do, since they are hypocrites who do not practice what they preach. He accuses them of placing huge burdens on others but being unwilling to lift a finger to help. He says everything they do is for the praise of others and self-congratulation. They're always looking for the best seat at banquets and in synagogues. They make their "phylacteries wide" and their "tassels long." Phylacteries were small boxes with Scripture passages inside, a literal way to obey the command to keep Scripture always in front of you (Ex 13:9, 16; Deut 6:8; 11:18). Putting tassels on garments was commanded in Numbers 15:38 and Deuteronomy 22:12 as a reminder of one's devotion to God. An extra large phylactery box told people you were quite the prayer warrior. With long tassels they could see from a distance just how spiritual you were. Today we might say someone carries a huge Bible to church to impress others or always talks about "the real meaning of this Greek word" to show off their Bible knowledge. Or perhaps they make a flashy show of placing a large bill in the offering basket so that everyone notices how "spiritual" they are. Jesus' point: it's all for show.

Jesus then pronounces a series of woes or judgment oracles against the Pharisees and the teachers of the law (Mt 23:13-36). Consider this small sampling:

> Woe to you, teachers of the law and Pharisees, you hypocrites! You shut the door of the kingdom of heaven in people's faces. You yourselves do not enter, nor will you let those enter who are trying to. (v.13)

> You travel over land and sea to win a single convert, and when you have succeeded, you make them twice as much a child of hell as you are. (v. 15)

> Woe to you, blind guides! . . . You blind fools! . . . You blind men! (vv. 16-17, 19)

> You give a tenth of your spices—mint, dill and cumin. But you have neglected the more important matters of the law—justice, mercy and faithfulness. (v. 23)

> You strain out a gnat but swallow a camel. (v. 24)

> You clean the outside of the cup and dish, but inside they are full of greed and self-indulgence. (v. 25)

> You are like whitewashed tombs, which look beautiful on the

> outside but on the inside are full of the bones of the dead and
> everything unclean. (v. 27)

> You build tombs for the prophets and decorate the graves of
> the righteous. . . . [But] you are the descendants of those who
> murdered the prophets. Go ahead, then, and complete what
> your ancestors started! (vv. 29, 31-32)

> You snakes! You brood of vipers! How will you escape being
> condemned to hell? (v. 33)

This is serious name-calling: hypocrites, blind guides, blind fools,
greedy, self-indulgent, murderers, sons of snakes! Instead of
training godly disciples, their converts become twice the "children
of hell" that they are (*Hell's Offspring*, sounds like a good title for a
horror movie). Instead of providing access to the kingdom, they are
slamming the door in people's faces. They look like pretty painted
tombs on the outside, but inside are full of putrid, decaying corpses
(another nice horror-movie touch). Instead of honoring God's
prophets, they murder them! Jesus does not seem very interested
in winning friends and influencing people. He looks more like an
angry iconoclast than a loving shepherd. *What's going on here?*

To comprehend Jesus' actions, we have to get to know the players
involved. This will help us understand who opposed Jesus and why
he lashed back so severely.

THE RELIGIOUS AND POLITICAL LANDSCAPE

During his early ministry in Galilee Jesus' conflict was primarily
with the Pharisees and the teachers of the law (the scribes). Though
we know very few specifics about the origin of the Pharisees as a
group, they likely arose from groups known as the *Hasidim* or "holy
ones," who supported the Maccabees against Antiochus Epiphanes
and his attempts to eradicate Judaism (see chap. 2). After the Jews
won their independence, the Pharisees gradually broke away from

the Maccabean rulers (known as the Hasmonean dynasty) when these rulers themselves began to openly adopt Hellenistic (i.e., Greek) culture and ways. The word *Pharisee* probably originally meant "separatist" and indicated separation *away* from pagan Hellenistic culture and *toward* God and his holiness. The Pharisees might best be compared to a political party today, except that in first-century Israel everything about politics was also religious, so they would be a political-religious party.

The primary political and religious opponents of the Pharisees were the Sadducees. The origin of the Sadducees is also shrouded in mystery, but they likely arose in opposition to the Pharisees as supporters of the Hasmonean dynasty. The Sadducees dominated the Sanhedrin, the Jewish ruling council, and the priestly temple leadership—the high priest and the priestly aristocracy. In this sense the Sadducees were political conservatives, supporters of the status quo. They were in power and intended to stay there.

The Sadducees and Pharisees also differed in their beliefs. The Pharisees believed in strict observance to the law of Moses, known as the Torah. They considered not only the written law to be authoritative but also the oral law or "traditions of the fathers"—additional rulings passed down for generations defining more specifically *how* the law should be kept. Today these rulings can be found in the Jewish Mishnah, a book about the size of the Bible full of comments and opinions by the rabbis. The Pharisees also believed in the coming of the Messiah, a king from the line of David who would establish God's kingdom and reign forever in righteousness and justice. They believed in the final resurrection, when God would raise the dead, reward the righteous and punish the wicked, and establish his eternal kingdom.

The Sadducees, by contrast, rejected many of these beliefs. They were not interested in a coming Messiah (since they were already at the top of the political heap) and did not believe in the resurrection of the dead. They believed in free will—you make of your life what you make of it—instead of fate or determinism.

While the Pharisees and Sadducees were political-religious parties, a scribe or teacher of the law was a profession or vocation. Scribes were experts in the law of Moses. They would teach in the synagogues and make rulings about the law for everyday life. One became a scribe not by ancestry (like the priests) or by joining a particular group (like the Pharisees and Sadducees), but by becoming a disciple or student of a respected rabbi and learning from him. Most scribes who were associated with a political party would have been Pharisees because of their common interest in and reverence for the Jewish law. Mark 2:16 refers to "teachers of the law [scribes] who were Pharisees."

Since the law was studied in the synagogues throughout Palestine, the Pharisees and scribes had their greatest influence in the towns and villages of Judea and Galilee. The Sadducees, by contrast, had their power base in Jerusalem, since that is where the temple with its priestly aristocracy was and where the Sanhedrin met. We might compare the Pharisees to local pastors or parish priests, while the Sadducees were big city bishops or cardinals, closer to the center of power.

CONFLICT IN GALILEE WITH THE PHARISEES AND SCRIBES

This brief summary shows that Jesus had much more in common with the scribes and the Pharisees than he did with the Sadducees. Like the Pharisees, he believed in the coming of the Messiah, the resurrection of the dead, the final judgment and the establishment of the kingdom of God. Like the Pharisees he viewed the whole of the Hebrew Scriptures (the Christian Old Testament) as the inspired Word of God. The Sadducees only treated the first five books, Genesis through Deuteronomy (known as the Pentateuch or Torah), as authoritative. If Jesus shared so much in common with the Pharisees, why did he have so much conflict with them?

First, as mentioned earlier, the issue was "turf." Just as in the game of *Risk*, they were both competing for the same real estate—the hearts and minds of the people in the villages and synagogue communities around Galilee. From the perspective of the Pharisees and scribes, Jesus was sheep stealing, drawing the people away from them and threatening their influence among the people.

Second, while Jesus and the Pharisees had the same foundational beliefs about God and his coming kingdom, they had radically different views about *how* God was bringing these promises to fulfillment. The Pharisees certainly expected God to intervene at some time in the future to raise up the Messiah and to establish his kingdom. Meanwhile, they sought to keep God's covenant through meticulous obedience to the law. The "sinners" who violated the law would be judged and cast into hell. The "righteous" who kept the law (the more meticulously the better) would be rewarded and blessed with a seat at the messianic banquet—God's great worker-appreciation picnic at the end of time (see Is 25:6-8).

Jesus had a radically different perspective. He claimed that through his own words and actions the kingdom was already breaking into human history and that *he himself* was God's agent of its arrival. He claimed his healings were snapshots of the promise of the creation's restoration (see Is 35:5-6). His exorcisms were evidence that God's kingdom was invading and overwhelming the kingdom of Satan. His resuscitations of dead people were previews of the end-time resurrection that would begin with his own resurrection from the dead. He also claimed that everyone—not just those deemed "sinners" by the religious leaders—must repent of their sins and respond in faith to the gospel, the good news of the kingdom. Salvation came as a free gift to those who believed.

From the perspective of the Pharisees and scribes, these were ludicrous claims that demanded a response. Imagine if someone showed up at your church and claimed to be the savior of the world. My father, who was a pastor, once had a man walk into church while he was preaching. He entered though a side entrance, walked right up to my dad, reached out his hand and said, "Hello, I'm Jesus Christ." Suspecting that the man was not who he said he was, my dad calmly asked if an usher would please escort the man to the back. In such a situation, a response was necessary. My father could not simply have said, "Would someone get Jesus a seat so we can worship him?"

In the same way, the religious leaders could not simply ignore this Galilean rabbi, with his adoring fans and provocative actions. Jesus' claim to be inaugurator of the kingdom of God demanded a response. He either was who he claimed to be or he was not. When the Pharisees and scribes rejected Jesus' claims about the kingdom, they had little choice but to condemn him at every turn: for claiming divine authority to forgive sins, for his lax attitude toward the Sabbath law and for hanging out with the wrong crowd. Although they couldn't deny that he had performed exorcisms, they accused him of doing them by Satan's power.

It becomes clear in this context why Jesus responded in such a forceful manner. He believed that his coming was the center point in human history, the climax of God's plan of salvation. There was no plan B. His mission was to call Israel to repentance and faith in preparation for the kingdom of God. Anyone who opposed this message stood in defiance of God. Jesus said, "Whoever is not with me is against me" (Mt 12:30//Lk 11:23). When the leaders of Israel rejected Jesus, he had no choice but to reject their authority and to publicly denounce them. He calls them "blind guides" because, from his perspective, that is what they were. They were leading Israel's people astray and missing out on God's plan of salvation—the climax of human history.

SHOWDOWN IN JERUSALEM

While Jesus' conflicts in Galilee were primarily with the Pharisees and their scribes, when he arrived in Jerusalem for the last Passover of his life, opposition came especially from the priestly leadership (the "chief priests") and the Sanhedrin. In Jesus' first prediction of his coming death (Mk 8:31//Mt 16:21//Lk 9:22), he said that he would be rejected by "the elders, the chief priests and the teachers of the law." These three groups composed the Sanhedrin, the Jewish high council. The *chief priests* were the priestly elite, made up of the high priest, his sons and other leading priests in Jerusalem. Most of them were probably members of the Sadducees, the party of the Jerusalem elite. The *elders* were likely lay leaders, the Jewish aristocracy in Jerusalem. As we have seen, the *teachers of the law* or *scribes* were experts in the law of Moses. Those referred to here were probably the most prestigious teachers who were also members of the Sanhedrin.

While Jesus may have been in danger at times in Galilee, the threat to him increased exponentially when he came to Jerusalem for his last Passover. Jerusalem was a volatile place at any time, but especially at Passover, when patriotic fervor ran high. The city's population would swell tenfold as Jewish pilgrims arrived from throughout the Roman Empire. Passover was a celebration of freedom, Israel's deliverance from slavery in Egypt. No one could miss the irony of squads of Roman soldiers—the present oppressors of Israel—overlooking the temple compound from their position on the Fortress of Antonia. Their threatening presence was a constant reminder that Israel was not free.

The Roman governor Pontius Pilate would come to Jerusalem for the festival to maintain crowd control. He was no doubt in a bad mood even before he arrived. To come to Jerusalem he had to leave the lush seaside resort of Caesarea Maritima (the Roman headquarters in Palestine), with its cool breezes and hot spas, and stay in the overcrowded oppressive city jammed with Jewish pilgrims. The din and smell of thousands of bleating sheep having their throats slit in preparation for Passover may have been a sweet aroma to the Jewish God, but for Pilate it was hell on earth. He would no doubt have had a very short fuse.

The Jewish priests overseeing the temple were also skittish at Passover, since any kind of disturbance was very bad for business. A Jewish prophet claiming to be God's agent of salvation was not their idea of a happy weekend. In this explosive context, three actions by Jesus were particularly provocative: his entrance into Jerusalem riding a donkey, his clearing of the temple, and his open debates with the religious leaders in the temple courts.

A royal entrance. All the evidence suggests Jesus intentionally provoked a crisis during this last Passover of his life. By entering Jerusalem riding a donkey (Mk 11:1-10//Mt 21:1-9//Lk 19:28-40//Jn 12:12-19) he appears to be purposely fulfilling Zechariah 9:9, a prophecy the Jews interpreted with reference to the coming Messiah:

> Rejoice greatly, Daughter Zion!
>   Shout, Daughter Jerusalem!
> See, your king comes to you,
>   righteous and victorious
> lowly and riding on a donkey,
>   on a colt, the foal of a donkey.

This is Jesus' first *public* affirmation that he is the Messiah. Pilgrims entering Jerusalem normally walked. For Jesus to intentionally send his disciples to procure a young donkey and then to ride it into Jerusalem—the only time in the Gospels he is portrayed as riding an animal—suggests an intentionally symbolic and provocative act. Even the action of procuring the donkey would have reminded first-century hearers of the ancient Near Eastern practice of impressment, whereby local citizens would be expected to supply anything needed for their king.

In John's Gospel we learn that the pilgrims are waving palm branches, a symbol of Jewish nationalism (Jn 12:13). What the pilgrims actually meant by their shouts of "Hosanna! Blessed is he who comes in the name of the Lord!" has been debated. *Hosanna* is Hebrew for "Save now!" and "he who comes in the name of the Lord" is from Psalm 118:26, one of the *Hallel* (praise) songs sung by pilgrims as they ascended to Jerusalem. In Mark's Gospel the crowd rejoices at the "coming kingdom of our father David" (Mk 11:10). In Luke they speak of "the king who comes in the name of the Lord" (Lk 19:38), and in Matthew, "the Son of David . . . who comes in the name of the Lord!" (Mt 21:9). In John, Jesus is called the "king of Israel" (Jn 12:13). All of these, together with the background of Zechariah 9:9, suggest that Jesus is making some kind of claim to be Israel's king, the promised Savior. This was an act that could not be ignored by the temple leadership.

Clearing the temple. The next act was even more provocative. Jesus entered the Jerusalem temple and drove out the moneychangers and sellers of animals (Mk 11:15-17//Mt 21:12-13//Lk 19:45-46; cf. Jn 2:13-17). Both of these groups played an essential role in the functioning of the temple. The moneychangers exchanged various currencies for the shekels produced in Tyre, which were required to pay the temple tax because of their consistent weight and value. The sellers provided animals for sacrifices for Jewish pilgrims. It was much easier for visitors to purchase animals at the temple, which were guaranteed kosher and suitable for sacrifice, than to bring them on their journey. Both the sellers and moneychangers would have been located in the outer court of the temple, the Court of the Gentiles.

If these were essential activities, why did Jesus cause such a ruckus? Jesus gives the answer by alluding to Jeremiah 7:11 and Isaiah 56:7: "'My house will be called a house of prayer for all nations.' But you have made it 'a den of robbers'" (Mk 11:17; cf. Mt 21:13//Lk 19:45-46). God's temple was a place of prayer and worship for all nations, and these activities were impeding this. The reference to "den of robbers" could perhaps mean that the sellers were extorting their customers by charging exorbitant prices. Yet the Greek word used here (*lēstai*) is not one usually used for swindlers or extortionists. It is more commonly used of roadside bandits or insurrections. Jesus is likely referring to the temple leadership, who are profiting through these activities and so impeding the worship of God.

This event is traditionally called the "Cleansing of the Temple," indicating that Jesus is purifying the temple from defilement. This would be similar to what Judas Maccabeus did when he rededicated the temple after its defilement by Antiochus Epiphanes. Jesus would be saying that the present leadership had defiled the temple and it needed to be purged or purified—a highly provocative act! While this may be part of Jesus' intention, it is likely that he is doing even more, symbolically judging and destroying the temple. Jesus will predict the destruction of the temple shortly after this (Mk 13:2//Mt 24:2//Lk 21:6; cf. Lk 19:43-44; Jn 2:19) and at his trial is accused of threatening to destroy it himself (Mk 14:58//Mt 26:61; Mk 15:29//Mt 27:40). His actions here may therefore be symbolically acting this out. Because of the failure of its corrupt leadership, the temple will be destroyed. Again, such an audacious challenge demanded a response.

Debating the Jerusalem leaders. After Jesus' actions in the temple, the Gospels describe a series of controversies between Jesus and the religious leaders (Mk 11:27–12:40; Mt 21:23–22:46; Lk 20:1-44). Each time Jesus defeats his opponents in debate and demonstrates his superior wisdom. Two episodes are particularly significant with reference to this confrontation.

First, a group of religious leaders—chief priests, scribes and elders—come to him and ask him by what authority he is doing these things (Mk 11:27-33//Mt 21:23-27//Lk 20:1-8). Jesus replies that he will answer that question if they will answer his own question: "John's baptism—was it from heaven, or of human origin?" The religious leaders see the trap. If they say "from heaven" (i.e., from God), then Jesus will say, "Why didn't you believe John when he pointed to me?" But if they say, "of human origin," the people will reject them, since they believed John to be a true prophet. Caught in a pickle, they confer among themselves and take the easy way out: "We don't know."

Ironically, by admitting their ignorance they concede their own illegitimacy. If the appointed leaders of Israel cannot discern a true prophet from a false one (in John's case), what claim do they have to speak for God with reference to Jesus? Jesus therefore refuses to answer: "Neither will I tell you by what authority I am doing these things." This is not simply a tit-for-tat answer. Jesus refuses to answer because in his view they have just admitted their disqualification to judge him. They have relinquished their role as Israel's leaders and judges. Of course in reality, they know that Jesus claims to be acting on God's behalf, but they refuse to admit this.

Immediately following this, Jesus tells the parable of the tenants, which again denies the legitimacy of Israel's religious leaders (Mk 12:1-12//Mt 21:33-46//Lk 20:9-19). In this allegorical parable, Jesus describes the religious leaders as tenant farmers who have the task of overseeing God's vineyard (representing Israel). When the owner of the vineyard (representing God) sends his servants (representing the prophets) to receive his share of the harvest, the tenants abuse, beat and murder them. The owner finally resolves to send his own son (Jesus), whom the tenants murder, throwing his body out of the vineyard.

The parable is a transparent allegory of Jesus' ministry, with the religious leaders portrayed as opponents of God who murder his prophets and eventually will murder his Son. With such an obvious parody, it is not surprising that the religious leaders of Israel view Jesus as a dangerous threat. Ominously, when Jesus finished telling this story, we learn that "the chief priests, the teachers of the law and the elders looked for a way to arrest him because they knew he had spoken the parable against them" (Mk 12:12). The great irony is that in taking steps to destroy him, they actually play out and fulfill their role in the parable.

With all of these actions—entering Jerusalem on a donkey, clearing the temple, challenging the religious leaders—Jesus is doing two things: (1) identifying himself as Israel's Messiah, and (2) intentionally provoking his own death.

Jesus' apparent "bad behavior"—his strong and severe language against the religious leaders—now makes sense in the context of his ministry. First, Jesus is acting as God's spokesperson and Israel's Messiah, announcing and inaugurating the kingdom of God and condemning the religious leaders for their failure to respond. Second, by challenging their legitimacy as leaders and shepherds of the nation, he is intentionally forcing their hand. They have no choice but to respond; they must either follow him or destroy him. Here is the great irony of the gospel story and the paradox of the cross. Through their rejection of God's anointed One, Israel's leaders in fact fulfill God's purpose. Salvation is accomplished through the sacrificial death of the Son.

CONCLUSION

I got a dose of humility a while back. My oldest son was about six or seven, just old enough to begin wondering and asking about what Dad did for a living. He asked me why people called me Dr. Strauss. I wasn't like others doctors he had met. Doctors were supposed to help you when you were sick. Dad wasn't much good at those times. In fact, Mom was much better. They should call *her* Dr. Strauss.

So I explained as best I could that what I had was a PhD, which made me a different kind of doctor from an MD. A PhD was an advanced degree, a specialist in a particular field. My field was New Testament and Greek. "Do you understand?" I asked. He half-nodded and said "uh huh" with that expression kids have when they have no clue what you're talking about.

A few weeks later we were watching TV together, and on the show someone referred to someone as a quack. My son said to me, "Dad, what's a quack?" I said, "Oh, that's someone who pretends to be a doctor, but really isn't." His eyes lit up and he said with a grin, "Oh, like you!"

Kids just don't have a lot of respect for high and mighty titles and degrees. What matters more to them is someone who is genuine and caring and willing to help. It's always fun to see the president of the United States visiting a school and getting an earful from a kindergartener who doesn't care that he's the most powerful man in the world.

Jesus' audacious mission was to fix a broken world, to bring humanity and all of creation back into a right relationship to God. He did not have time or patience with the doctors and lawyers of religious law, who elevated themselves above others and rejected his announcement of the kingdom. His strong rebukes of them must be understood in this context.

When Jesus called Levi, a tax collector, to be his disciple and then accepted an invitation to a celebratory banquet at his home, the religious leaders scoffed. "Why does he eat with tax collectors and sinners?" Jesus answered with a proverb and then a profound explanation: "It is not the healthy who need a doctor, but the sick. I have not come to call the righteous, but sinners" (Mk 2:17; cf. Mt 9:13//Lk 5:32). The religious leaders did not think they needed a doctor, because in their eyes they were not sick. They had earned their righteousness. Jesus' call to repent and submit to God's kingdom fell on deaf ears. By contrast, the poor, the sinners, the tax collectors and prostitutes recognized their brokenness and responded to Jesus' message with faith and gratitude.

God is not impressed with a PhD. He's not impressed with extraordinary athletic ability or scientific knowledge or the entrepreneurial skills to make billions of dollars. He's not impressed by great oratory skills or the charms of a great politician able to wow the masses. What impresses him instead is a humble heart of dependence, a childlike faith in him. Jesus said,

> Let the little children come to me, and do not hinder them, for the kingdom of God belongs to such as these. Truly I tell you, anyone who will not receive the kingdom of God like a little child will never enter it. (Mk 10:14-15)

Environmentalist or Earth Scorcher?

Killing Pigs and Cursing Trees

I have come to bring fire on the earth,
and how I wish it were already kindled!

Jesus of Nazareth, Luke 12:49

MICHAEL VICK IS A REMARKABLE ATHLETE. After an exceptional college career as quarterback for Virginia Tech, he was selected first overall in the 2001 NFL draft by the Atlanta Falcons. Vick played six seasons for the Falcons and during that time was selected to three Pro Bowls. Twice he led the Falcons to the playoffs. As a running quarterback Vick was explosive on the field, often turning what looked to be a loss of yardage into big gains. He was enormously popular with the fans.

Then scandal hit. In April 2007 Vick was implicated in an illegal dog-fighting ring. He was revealed to be a major sponsor of the Bad Newz Kennels, which housed and trained fifty pit bulls, staged dog fights, killed dogs and ran a high stakes gambling ring. For days the story led the evening news, highlighting pictures of abused and battered dogs. It was now Vick's turn to experience abuse. The vitriol against him was deafening. While the American public can forgive its celebrities almost any transgression—from dabbling in drugs to cavorting with prostitutes—cruelty to defenseless animals was just too much. Product endorsements were canceled and Vick's popularity plunged. In August 2007 he pleaded guilty to felony charges and served twenty-one months in prison. Once the NFL's highest paid player, Vick filed for bankruptcy in July 2008.

In America we love our animals, especially our dogs. Anyone who would hurt, maim or kill a dog is forever, well, in the doghouse. While Vick's career has been gradually rehabilitated through lots of contrition, public service and the passage of time, he will forever be known as the man who abused dogs. A case in point, when writing this section, I mentioned Vick to my wife (not a football follower). Her first response: "Oh, the dog killer!"

Senseless seems to be the right word for abusing animals. When I was ten years old my mom got a frantic call from our next-door neighbor. She had seen a snake in their front yard and was too terrified to leave the house. My brother and I went out to investigate and to save this damsel in distress. After a brief search we found the snake moving across the front yard. It was a harmless garter snake. It had beautiful coral skin and moved effortlessly across the ground through a complex series of muscle contractions. We admired its amazing beauty and grace—a marvelous creation of God. Then we chopped its head off.

To this day I regret that senseless act of violence. We could have easily caught the snake and released it into the woods. But we were young and stupid. There, I've confessed my sin. My foolishness might be forgiven because I was just a kid, squashing bugs for no reason and blowing up plastic model airplanes with firecrackers. But imagine the publicity nightmare for Jesus when word got out that he had caused the senseless death of an entire herd of pigs. The paparazzi would be waiting at his door.

CRUELTY TO ANIMALS? THE SWINE GO SWIMMING

RABBI JESUS CAUSES THE DEATH OF 2000 PIGS: OUTRAGED HERDSMEN LAUNCH PROTEST

This might have been the headline in the *Galilean Gazette* following the incident described in Mark 5:1-20 (//Mt 8:28-34//Lk 8:26-39). It is one of the strangest in the Gospels.

The context: A storm at sea. Jesus and his disciples have just crossed the Sea of Galilee by boat, traveling from the Jewish region on the northwest shore to a Gentile region on the southeast. The trip itself had already been eventful. As they crossed the lake, a powerful storm struck. Jesus, exhausted from a long day of ministry, was asleep on a cushion in the stern. When the boat began to be swamped in the storm, the disciples feared for their lives and cried out for help. Jesus awoke, got up, rebuked the wind and said to the waves, "Quiet! Be still!" Immediately the wind stopped and the sea became calm (Mk 4:39).

If this story doesn't make you gulp, you've been going to Sunday school too long. ("Yeah, yeah, the Red Sea parted, the walls of Jericho fell down, Jesus calmed the sea—whatever.") The flabbergasted disciples are terrified and respond, "Who is this? Even the wind and the waves obey him!" (Mk 4:41).

The point of the story is, of course, Jesus' amazing authority. In the Old Testament, God alone controls the forces of nature. Psalm 89:9 reads, "You rule over the surging sea; / when its waves mount up, you still them." Psalm 107:23-29 is even more descriptive:

Some went out on the sea in ships; . . .
They saw the works of the LORD;
    his wonderful deeds in the deep.
For he spoke and stirred up a tempest
    that lifted high the waves. . . .

They reeled and staggered like drunkards;
   they were at their wits' end.
Then they cried out to the LORD in their trouble,
   and he brought them out of their distress.
He stilled the storm to a whisper;
   the waves of the sea were hushed.

Jesus' calming of the sea sounds like a play reenacting this psalm. The disciples go to sea, a storm rises, they cry out to Jesus, and he stills the storm. The point is clear: Jesus is acting with the authority of God. There may be something more here as well. In the ancient Near East the sea often symbolized a place of chaos, evil and destruction. The fact that Jesus "rebukes" the sea, just as he rebukes demons (Mk 1:25; 9:25), indicates his power to defeat the forces of evil. This theme is important to the scene that follows.

Arrival in Gerasa. When the boat arrives at the southeastern shore of the lake, more adventure awaits the disciples. They come ashore near a graveyard and a wild-looking, demon-possessed man emerges from the tombs. The Gospel writer Mark loves a good story and often provides the most vivid and colorful descriptions. He does not disappoint here:

> This man lived in the tombs, and no one could bind him anymore, not even with a chain. For he had often been chained hand and foot, but he tore the chains apart and broke the irons on his feet. No one was strong enough to subdue him. Night and day among the tombs and in the hills he would cry out and cut himself with stones. (Mk 5:3-5)

Luke adds that for a long time the guy had worn no clothes (Lk 8:27). The only thing worse than a violent, demon-possessed lunatic is a *naked*, violent, demon-possessed lunatic. When my wife and I lived in Scotland during my doctoral studies, a Scottish friend was telling us about the fearsome reputation of the Scottish highlanders in battle (ever seen the movies *Braveheart* or *Rob Roy*?). He said, "People talk about the Scots fighting in kilts, but in fact, one reason they were so terrifying is that in battle they would throw off their kilts and fight naked." I had to admit that was a terrifying thought, a naked Scot charging at me with a battle ax.

Well, Jesus is facing worse: a demon-possessed, naked lunatic charging at him. This makes the next scene shocking—and also comical. The demon-possessed man comes to a screeching halt right in front of Jesus. They face off, but who falls on his face and screams in terror? The demon! It cries out, "What do you want with me, Jesus, Son of the Most High God! In God's name don't torture me!" (Mk 5:7). As so often in the Gospels, when a demon encounters Jesus, it is the demon, not Jesus, who is terrified, because it knows who Jesus is and why he has come. He is here to restore creation, to reverse the deception of Satan and to take back those held in spiritual captivity.

From a Jewish perspective, everything about this scene is repulsive and defiling. This is a Gentile region, which itself was defiling to a pious Jew. Tombs were ceremonially unclean because of the presence of dead bodies. Demons were called "unclean" or "impure" spirits because of their defiling presence. Nakedness was humiliating and shameful.

Yet Jesus is about to bring healing and purity to this unclean scene. The good news of the kingdom is salt and light, transforming and restoring all that it touches.

The exorcism. Jesus asks the demon's name and it replies, "My name is Legion." A legion was a Roman regiment of about six thousand troops. This doesn't mean that there were six thousand demons. The point is, as the demon itself says, "we are many" (Mk 5:9). Such a massive demonic force should represent a huge challenge for Jesus, but as usual he is fully in charge. In Mark's Gospel the demon begs Jesus not to cast them "out of the area." The demons evidently think that they will lose their authority if forced out of their present region (see Mt 12:43-45). In Luke's version of the account the demon begs Jesus not to send them "into the Abyss" (Lk 8:31). The New Testament speaks elsewhere of some demons that are held in captivity and unable to roam the earth (2 Pet 2:4; cf. Rev 9:1-2, 11; 11:7; 17:8; 20:1, 3). The demons likely fear that Jesus will send them into this place of captivity or somewhere else where they will be powerless. So they beg him instead to send them into a large herd of pigs.

Surprisingly, Jesus agrees. This is puzzling. Why would Jesus negotiate with a demon? Why not just say, "Shut up and get out!" like he does elsewhere (see Mk 1:25)? A possible answer may come from Matthew's parallel passage, where the demons say, "Have you come here to torture us *before the appointed time?*" (Mt 8:29). The "appointed time" is the final day of judgment. So the demon is saying, "Hey, you're jumping the gun. It's not judgment day yet!" So Jesus gives a temporary stay of execution by sending the demons into the pigs. The irony is that it *is* judgment day, because the power of the kingdom of God is already at work in Jesus' words and deeds. This is played out in the events that follow.

When the demons enter the pigs, the pigs are startled and rush down the hillside into the sea and are drowned. Mark tells us there were two thousand pigs! That's a lot of pork. What happened to the demons at the death of the pigs is not explained. It is possible, of course, that they were now free to roam the earth and find other victims. But this is unlikely, since it would imply a win for them. Whenever Jesus encounters demons, they lose. Here, though the demons think they've gotten the best of Jesus, their gamble doesn't pay off and they are rendered powerless. The death of the pigs likely sends them to the very place of captivity they feared the most—the Abyss. As noted earlier, ancient peoples viewed the sea as a place of chaos, darkness and destruction. The irony, then, is that the demons get what they deserve. Jesus agrees to their request, but it ultimately leads to their demise.

Those tending the pigs, gaping at this scene of carnage, rush terrified into town and tell the townspeople what Jesus has done. They all come out and beg Jesus to leave. If this strange and powerful exorcist can do such damage to their herds, what might he do to them?

A senseless loss of life? The passage raises several ethical questions. First, how could Jesus allow such a horrific loss of animal life? Is this cruelty to the pigs justified? And what about the enormous loss of revenue for the owner(s) of the herd? A herd this size was worth a small fortune, and Jesus has apparently caused its destruction. Is this an example of Jesus behaving badly?

A closer look teaches us a great deal about his identity and his mission. First, it is not clear that Jesus knew what would happen to the pigs. During his earthly life, Jesus didn't know everything (Mk 13:32//Mt 24:36), and so he was not necessarily aware what the demons would do to the pigs. Second and more important, however, Jesus did not kill the pigs; the demons did. The mass drowning is not so much about the recklessness of Jesus as the destructive power of Satan and his forces. While God is the giver of life, the devil "was a murderer from the beginning" (Jn 8:44). He "prowls around like a roaring lion looking for someone to devour" (1 Pet 5:8).

Third, and closely related to this, the story illustrates the very real spiritual struggle that is going on in Jesus' ministry. God is at war with Satan, and there are casualties in this war. When we see the deaths of innocent people caused by wars and famines and even so-called natural disasters, people sometimes blame God. But this world is a fallen place—a result of human sin—and people and things suffer because of humanity's rejection of God. All disease, death and destruction is unnatural in the sense that it is a result of human brokenness and is contrary to God's original design for his good creation.

When seen from this perspective, Jesus' actions carry positive theological and symbolic significance. His mastery over demons—even such a massive "army" of them—confirms that he is the Lord's Anointed, who brings victory over Satan and the forces of evil. While the demons wreak destruction, Jesus brings healing and hope. The fact that this is done in a Gentile region also has symbolic significance. The healing and restoration that Jesus brings is not just for Israel but for the Gentile nations as well.

The reaction of the herders and the townspeople also illustrates various responses to the kingdom of God and God's offer of salvation. The townspeople come upon a scene of stark contrasts. On the one side they see the pigs, a scene of chaos and carnage. On the other side, they see this formerly deranged and demon-possessed man sitting calmly and in his right mind, an amazing miracle of God. On the one side, a *person* is restored. On the other, *property* is destroyed. Which scene will they embrace? Instead of responding with joy and acceptance to the awesome power of God, they respond with fear and rejection at their loss.

Contrast this with the man's response. He is healed and in his right mind, "sitting at Jesus' feet" (Lk 8:35), the position of a disciple (Lk 10:39; Acts 22:3 NRSV). While the townspeople beg Jesus to leave, the man begs Jesus for the privilege of following him. Then, when Jesus sends him home instead, he becomes a messenger of the good news, proclaiming everywhere "how much God had done for [him]" (Mk 5:19//Lk 8:39).

This is not a case of Jesus acting recklessly. It is an epic battle scene in the spiritual war that is being waged for the hearts and souls of people throughout the Galilee.

CURSING A FIG TREE

If the death of the pigs seems like an arbitrary action inappropriate for Jesus, the cursing and withering of a fig tree may be even worse, since it was performed directly by Jesus. The episode is recorded in Matthew and Mark (Mt 21:18-22//Mk 11:12-14, 20-26). Luke omits it, perhaps because he tells a parable about a barren fig tree earlier and does not want to duplicate it (Lk 13:6-9). Or he may have been uncomfortable with the scene in the same way many readers today are.

The context is the last week of Jesus' life. Jesus has arrived in Jerusalem for the Passover celebration. It's Monday morning, the morning after Jesus' triumphal entry into Jerusalem. He's staying just outside the city in the village of Bethany, an eastern suburb of Jerusalem just over the hill known as the Mount of Olives. Each morning Jesus comes into Jerusalem to teach in the temple.

As Jesus is leaving Bethany in the morning, he sees a fig tree with leaves on it. Leaves indicate the possibility of fruit. He's hungry and goes to investigate. Yet when he finds no fruit, he pronounces a curse on the tree, "May no one ever eat fruit from you again." He curses the tree! To make matters worse, Mark tells us that it wasn't even the season for figs. Jesus condemns the tree even though it wasn't the tree's fault.

I'm sometimes in a bad mood when I haven't had any breakfast in the morning and my blood sugar is low, especially on a Monday. I'm even worse when I haven't had my coffee. Don't cut me off on the freeway before my morning coffee. I might just curse your fig tree. (Maybe this is the cause of all that road rage in Los Angeles, low blood sugar and caffeine withdrawal.) Was Jesus having a bad Monday because of low blood sugar? We might expect such a fit of temper from us sinners, but surely the Son of God should have better self-control!

The scene gets even worse. According to Mark's Gospel, the next day Jesus and the disciples are returning to Jerusalem and they discover that the fig tree has withered from the roots. The curse worked! While this certainly shows Jesus' power, it also makes him look like a petty tyrant who vents his anger on innocent victims. In Matthew's version the fig tree "withers at once." This apparent discrepancy is quite easily resolved. The fig tree probably withered very shortly after Jesus' curse, but the disciples did not discover it until the next morning. Matthew is famous for abbreviating episodes in this way.[1]

This is the only example in the Gospels of a miracle of destruction. Many people have found the whole scene rather small-minded and vindictive, inappropriate for a man of Jesus' stature. T. W. Manson, one of the great British New Testament scholars of a previous generation, doubted the story's authenticity: "It is a tale of miraculous power wasted in the service of ill temper (for the supernatural energy employed to blast the unfortunate tree might have been more usefully expended in forcing a crop of figs out of season); and as it stands it is simply incredible."[2]

Manson decided that what Jesus actually meant was not a curse but a prediction. No one would eat fruit from the tree again because of the coming destruction of Jerusalem. The whole region, with its people and crops, would be devastated. The problem with this interpretation is that Jerusalem was not destroyed for another forty years!

As noted in chapter one, Bertrand Russell, in his famous essay "Why I Am Not a Christian," pointed to this passage as evidence that Jesus was not so great after all.

> This is a very curious story, because it was not the right time of year for figs, and you really could not blame the tree. I cannot myself feel that either in the matter of wisdom or in the matter of virtue Christ stands quite as high as some other people known to history. I think I should put Buddha and Socrates above Him in those respects.[3]

In other words, Russell rejected Christianity as a religion because of Jesus' capricious actions like this. So what's going on here? Is Jesus behaving badly?

Symbolic judgment against Israel. Mark's Gospel, the earliest of the four, gives us the best clue about the significance of Jesus' actions. Mark intentionally places the event in one of his famous "intercalations" or sandwich structures. This sandwich or framing technique is where one episode begins (the bread on the bottom of the sandwich) and is then interrupted by another one (the meat in the middle) before it finishes (the bread on the top). The two episodes mutually interpret one another. For example, Mark sandwiches the Beelzebul episode, where the religious leaders accuse Jesus of casting out demons by Satan's power, between two episodes related to Jesus' family (Mk 3:20-35). The rejection of Jesus by his own family symbolically mirrors the rejection by his own people, the leaders of Israel. This sandwiching technique can also be used to set episodes in contrast to one another. Jesus' trial before the Sanhedrin is sandwiched between the beginning and end of the account of Peter's denial (Mk 14:53-72). Jesus' faithfulness to his mission is set in contrast to Peter's unfaithful denial that he even knows Jesus. Many of Mark's most important themes are highlighted through this literary device.

The present episode is probably Mark's most famous sandwich. Jesus curses the fig tree, then enters Jerusalem and clears the temple. Later, the fig tree is discovered withered (Mk 11:12-26). The sandwich structure indicates that the withering of the tree, like the temple clearing, represents God's judgment against Israel for the nation's unbelief.

There are many indications that this is Jesus' intention. First, symbolic actions like this are common in the prophets (1 Kings 11:29-31; Is 8:1-4; 20:1-6; Ezek 4:1-15; Hos 1:2). The prophet Jeremiah especially used objects—linen belts, clay pots, wooden yokes—to illustrate Israel's unfaithfulness and God's coming judgment (Jer

13:1-11; 19:1-13; 27:1-22). On one occasion God told Jeremiah to purchase a clay pot from the potter and to shatter it at the gates of Jerusalem in front of the leading priests and elders (Jer 19:1-13). The
broken pot symbolized that God would bring judgment against
Judah and Jerusalem at the hands of the Babylonians because of
Israel's sins.

Fig trees are also common in judgment oracles in the Old Testament (Is 28:4; Jer 8:13; 24:1-10; 29:17; Hos 2:12; 9:10, 16-17; Mic 7:1).
More specifically, figs and grapes are used to illustrate spiritual unfruitfulness. Hosea pronounced God's judgment because of Israel's
unfruitfulness. Ephraim, the largest tribe of the northern kingdom
of Israel, is used here as another name for Israel:

> "Ephraim is blighted,
>   their root is withered,
>   they yield no fruit.
> Even if they bear children,
>   I will slay their cherished offspring."
> My God will reject them
>   because they have not obeyed him;
>   they will be wanderers among the nations.
> (Hos 9:16-17; see also Mic 7:1)

Israel's unfruitfulness will result in judgment. The most
famous example of this theme is the Song of the Vineyard in
Isaiah 5:1-7. The passage begins as a love song, where God celebrates his care and concern for his vineyard, symbolizing Israel.
He planted his beloved vineyard on a fertile hillside, cleared it
of stones, used the best vines, and built a wall and watchtower
for its protection. Yet the vineyard produced only bad fruit. In
response God will tear down its wall and allow it to be trampled.
It will become a wasteland. The interpretation of the parable is
then given:

> The vineyard of the LORD Almighty
>> is the nation of Israel,
> and the people of Judah
>> are the vines he delighted in.
> And he looked for justice, but saw bloodshed;
>> for righteousness, but heard cries of distress. (Is 5:7)

There is a play on words here, since the Hebrew words for "justice" and "bloodshed" sound alike, and the Hebrew words for "righteousness" and "cries of distress" also sound alike. In the context of Isaiah's prophecies the meaning of the parable is that God will remove his divine protection from Israel and will allow the armies of Assyria to sweep in and devastate the nation. In this way God will judge his people for their sin.

Significantly, just a few paragraphs after the cursing of the fig tree, Jesus will tell the parable of the wicked tenant farmers (Mk 12:1-12//Mt 21:33-46//Lk 20:9-19). In this parable Jesus adapts Isaiah's Song of the Vineyard to a new context. As we have seen (see chap. 3), Jesus here portrays Israel's leaders as wicked tenant farmers over God's vineyard, whom God will judge because they have failed to provide the owner (God) his share of the crop. They have rejected and abused the owner's messengers (the prophets) and have finally killed the owner's son (Jesus himself).

In this larger context, Jesus' cursing of the fig tree seems clearly to be a symbolic act signifying coming judgment against Jerusalem and the temple. This is not a temper tantrum by an angry child. It is an enacted parable by God's spokesperson. Israel's leaders are rejecting Jesus' announcement of the kingdom of God and so will suffer the same consequences as Israel in Isaiah's day—the judgment of God.

But what about Mark's statement that "it was not the season for figs"? Why would Jesus look for fruit if there could not have been any? One possibility is the one just given—that Jesus is simply teaching an object lesson. He knows there will be no fruit but wants to act out this parable. This is certainly possible, but it seems to make Jesus a bit disingenuous. Mark explicitly says Jesus was hungry and so "he went to find out if it had any fruit." Was he simply play-acting for the disciples?

Another possibility relates to the fruit cycle of the fig tree. The common fig tree (*ficus carica*) generally produces two crops a year. A first or "breva" crop comes in the spring and is produced on the previous year's growth sprout. These are called "early figs" (Is 28:4; Jer 24:2; Hos 9:10; Mic 7:1). They are harder and less edible than the later figs. The main figs, which are better in quantity and quality, develop from the current year's growth and produce in late summer or fall. Since Jesus is present at Passover in the spring, he is looking for some of the early fruit.

Mark may actually hint at this in the way he describes the situation. While the NIV translates that Jesus went to find out if the tree had "any fruit," the Greek actually says he went to see if it had "anything" (*ti*) on it. Perhaps Mark means that Jesus came to the tree looking for "something" (i.e., early figs), because he knew it was not yet the time for the main harvest (i.e., late figs).

Either of these solutions is possible. But in either case we must not miss the primary point. Jesus is not throwing a low-blood-sugar-induced Monday morning tantrum against an innocent tree. He is rather acting in the tradition of the Hebrew prophets before him, pronouncing judgment against Israel for its failure to respond to God's Word.

More than a prophet: A new temple and a new way to God. Yet what is unique about Jesus' actions must also not be missed. While prophets like Isaiah and Jeremiah pronounced judgment against Israel and even predicted the coming destruction of Jerusalem, Jesus is doing much more. He is both the herald and inaugurator of

God's *final salvation*, the coming of the kingdom of God. Not only will the temple be destroyed but Jesus himself will become the foundation of a new temple.

Jesus indicates this in the episode that follows. Following the parable of the tenant farmers, Jesus quotes from Psalm 118:22-23 to explain its significance:

> The stone the builders rejected
>   has become the cornerstone;
> the Lord has done this,
>   and it is marvelous in our eyes. (Mk 12:10-11//Mt 21:42//
>   Lk 20:17)

Though Jesus will be a rejected stone, from this "cornerstone" God himself will raise up a new temple. It will be a spiritual temple, not built by human hands. It will be made up of the people of God, the body of Christ (cf. 1 Cor 3:16; 2 Cor 6:16; Eph 2:21). The animal sacrifices of the Jerusalem temple will cease, and Jesus' sacrificial death on the cross will become the once-and-for-all sacrifice for sins (see Heb 10:11-14). The renewal that begins with his resurrection will continue through his body, the church, which is the new temple of God. Again, Jesus' apparently "bad behavior" is meant to teach something profound about his identity and mission.

CONCLUSION: AN ENVIRONMENTAL IMPACT REPORT

In this chapter we have examined two of Jesus' most puzzling actions, sending a herd of pigs to drown in the sea and cursing a fig tree, causing it to wither and die. These have sometimes been viewed as wanton acts of destruction or childish fits of temper, unbefitting a wise and goodhearted teacher. Worse yet, they seem to express a general disregard for God's good creation. Does Jesus not see value in animals and plants? Shouldn't we be caretakers of God's creation rather than its destroyers?

Christians are often seen as caring little for the environment. Conservative political tendencies, often motivated by social and ethical concerns, have tended to ally believers with a broader conservative political agenda. This agenda, in turn, emphasizes economic expansion, free markets, private enterprise and a progrowth agenda. In this political environment the Genesis command to "subdue" the earth (Gen 1:28) can sometimes be taken as an excuse to exploit the earth's resources for short-term economic gain, without concern for its environmental impact. Salvation can be so spiritualized that concern for the world and its ecosystems is treated as of little significance. The important thing is to "save souls," not to save the panda, protect the ozone or prevent global warming. "This world is not our home," we sometimes hear, or "It's all going to burn anyway" or "Christ is coming to lay waste this world and start over with a new one."

Seen through this lens, Jesus' actions may seem to show little regard for the environment. What value, after all, do animals or plants have in comparison to Jesus' mission to pay the penalty for sins and to save our souls?

Yet such a narrow perspective misses the global significance of Jesus' announcement of the kingdom of God and the coming restoration of God's good creation. The physical world is a good thing, and God created its beauty and bounty to be enjoyed, tended and cared for, not destroyed.

This brings us to the heart of the gospel. Jesus came not just to save souls but to bring restoration to a fallen world. He came to establish the kingdom of God, which means to bring about the renewal of creation promised by Isaiah and the prophets. At that time, Isaiah predicts, the blind will see, the lame will walk, the deaf will hear; "water will gush forth in the wilderness / and streams in the desert" (Is 35:5-6). This is environmental renewal at its best! There will be no war or killing. The nations

will beat their swords into plowshares
> and their spears into pruning hooks.
Nation will not take up sword against nation,
> nor will they train for war anymore. (Is 2:4)

At that time,

> The wolf will live with the lamb,
> > the leopard will lie down with the goat,
> the calf and the lion and the yearling together;
> > and a little child will lead them.
> The cow will feed with the bear,
> > their young will lie down together,
> > and the lion will eat straw like the ox.
> The infant will play near the cobra's den,
> > the young child will put its hand into the viper's nest.
> They will neither harm nor destroy
> > on all my holy mountain,
> for the earth will be filled with the knowledge of the LORD
> > as the waters cover the sea. (Is 11:6-9; cf. Is 65:25)

This is a vision of renewal and restoration, of beauty and peace
and reconciliation. This was Jesus' vision for the future. In chapter
two I noted that Jesus' miracles were not only individual acts of
compassion but also signs that his kingdom would be one of restoration, healing, wholeness and peace. This is his overall goal for all
of creation—physical and spiritual. And it is a vision that Christians
ought to embrace. We need to celebrate God's good creation and
long for its renewal. We don't just say, "It's all going to hell." Instead,
we do what we can to counter the effects of evil, however it mani-
fests itself today. Just as we seek to alleviate the results of the fall in
other respects—like battling crime, poverty and hunger and seeking
cures for disease—so we ought to counter the fallen human ten-

dency to exploit and destroy God's good earth. Creation care is a *Christian* cause.

To be sure, this vision of a restored creation can only be ultimately realized if its fundamental causes are addressed. There is more wrong with this world than dirty water and climate change. The social and spiritual gospels are inseparable. For true restoration to take place, our fallen human nature must be renewed. That's where Jesus' mission to Jerusalem and journey to the cross comes in. The cursing and withering of the fig tree symbolize God's judgment—judgment Jesus would ultimately take upon himself.

Restoration for a broken world. Once, after I spoke at a church service, two teenage girls came to the front to speak with me. One of them was struggling with her faith. She said she simply couldn't believe in a God who commanded the killing of innocent animals. From her perspective, this was cruelty to animals. Of course we would have to include Jesus in this indictment, since he implicitly affirmed the animal sacrifices commanded in the Old Testament (Mt 5:23; Mk 1:44//Mt 8:4//Lk 5:14; Mk 14:12//Lk 22:7).

I was tempted to downplay the animal sacrifices of the Bible. I thought about saying, "Well they killed them very humanely by slitting their throats, without much pain." Or I might have pointed out that most animals sacrificed were also eaten for food. Unless you believe all carnivores, like lions and tigers, are acting out of malice, the killing for food can hardly be called morally wrong. Or I could have been more cynical and asked if she ever ate steak or hamburger or chicken sandwiches or even fish. These foods don't grow on trees. Unless you are a vegan (she may have been), the eating of any meat results in animal death.

Instead I took a different tack. I said something like, "Yes, that's a terrible thing, isn't it? Animal death, like human death, is a tragedy. Something is clearly wrong." We went on to talk about how we live in a broken world, where death is a result of our fallenness. It is caused by wars and murders and disease and "natural" disasters. But none of these things is natural or right. They are all the result of life in a broken and sinful world. The commands in the Bible to offer animal sacrifices were intended as a reminder of our fallen condition and the serious consequence of sin. They were meant to remind us of God's perfect justice and that every evil and wrong must be made right.

Jesus came to bring about God's justice by taking these consequences upon himself. He spoke of his own death as an atoning sacrifice for the sin (Mk 10:45//Mt 20:28). The early Christians recognized his life, death and resurrection as a once-for-all sacrifice for the sins of the world, reversing the results of the fall and launching the restoration of creation.

In this new creation,

> The wolf will live with the lamb,
>   the leopard will lie down with the goat. . . .
> They will neither harm nor destroy
>   on all my holy mountain,
> for the earth will be filled with the knowledge of the LORD
>   as the waters cover the sea. (Is 11:6, 9)

This is the vision of the world that the young woman I spoke with that evening was hoping for. And she was right! This is God's vision for the world as well.

Legalist or Grace Filled?

Be Perfect . . . or Else?

*Grace is a message of unconditional love from the Father of
the universe. . . . And we can experience it all in the
gritty now as well as in the sweet by and by.*

Dudley Hall, *Grace Works*

Legalism can be a destructive force in people's
lives. As I'm writing this chapter a scandal continues to unfold in
the news related to Bill Gothard's ministry, the Institute in Basic
Life Principles (IBLP).[1] Over thirty women have come forward
with claims of sexual harassment against Gothard. While these
charges are by far the most serious that have been leveled against
this ministry, for years former members and participants of IBLP
and its affiliate ATI (Advanced Training Institute) have complained
about the negative consequences of the legalistic lifestyle promoted by the group. The website recoveringgrace.org launched in
2011 has documented many of these stories.

Since the 1960s millions have attended Gothard's seminars.

Many have claimed the principles taught in the seminars have transformed their lives in a positive way. The call for modesty in dress, honoring parents, Bible study and family time together resonates with Christians who have felt besieged by the increasingly hostile culture around them. Alissa Wilkinson, college professor and film critic for *Christianity Today*, attended ATI seminars as a teen. She writes,

> A lot of ATI's practices seem refreshingly old-fashioned and wholesome, especially to those who are more familiar with broken families, angry teenagers, and destructive lifestyles. For instance: Families enrolled in ATI gathered around their kitchen tables for "Wisdom Searches" in the morning (a type of exegetical study of the Proverbs) and learned songs about character qualities, complete with hand motions. They committed to not using birth control and filling their "quivers" with children.
>
> They did not listen to "rock music" (any music with an emphasis on beats two and four, which ranges from country to jazz to CCM to actual rock 'n roll), drink alcohol, dance, or wear worldly clothing (especially blue jeans). They threw away their Cabbage Patch Dolls (which were reportedly at least possibly imbued with a Satanic spirit—why risk it?), eschewed youth groups, and committed to "courtship" (a parent-driven and orchestrated method for getting to the altar) instead of dating. They learned Biblical vocabulary words, like "diligence" and "courage," and also "grace," which was defined, perhaps tellingly, not in the traditional Protestant way (which often reiterated that grace was freely given and undeserved by the recipient) but as "the desire and the power to do God's will."[2]

There is, of course, nothing wrong (and much right) with setting high standards to live by. The Bible says a great deal about living in obedience to God and his righteous standards. Yet such practices become legalism when people insist that you live up to *their* standards in areas that are not explicitly moral or biblical. For example, ATI principles discouraged students from going to college (where they might be exposed to secular humanism and liberal professors); men were told not to grow facial hair (which "obscured the countenance"); and women were encouraged to grow their hair long and to style it with soft curls.[3]

Legalism is also claiming God won't love you unless you act a certain way and that your value to God, and even your salvation, depends on living by these rules. Legalism is shame based rather than grace based. One former ATI student writes of her experience since leaving the organization:

> Over the past 15 years, I've gradually learned that God doesn't dislike me. He is always present and active, gentle and loving. When I sin, there is much grace. When I succeed, there is much grace. When I'm apathetic and can't bring myself to "try" any harder, His grace is still there with me. Grace is so much more than "the power and desire to do God's will." It's God Himself, carrying me whether I walk or stumble. It's completely undeserved—God's unmerited favor.[4]

So where did Gothard get his teaching? I'm sure he would say from the Bible and Jesus himself. So, was Jesus a legalist? What do we learn in the Gospels?

WAS JESUS A LEGALIST?

It is clear that Jesus called his listeners to a high standard. In the Sermon on the Mount, for example, he taught that "unless your righteousness surpasses that of the Pharisees and the teachers of the law, you will certainly not enter the kingdom of heaven" (Mt 5:19-20). He apparently demanded perfection from his followers: "Be perfect . . . as your heavenly Father is perfect" (Mt 5:48). The Old

Testament law was hard enough to keep, but Jesus upped the ante, saying that anger was equivalent to murder and lust was a form of adultery (Mt 5:21-22, 27-28). After healing a lame man, he commanded him to stop sinning "or something worse may happen to you" (Jn 5:14). This sounds like a threat! How could anyone hope to live up to these impossible standards?

Jesus also taught that salvation was something difficult to attain. When asked, "Are only a few people going to be saved?" he responded, "Make every effort to enter through the narrow door, because many, I tell you, will try to enter and will not be able to" (Lk 13:22-24; cf. Mt 7:13-14). He also said, "Many are called, but few *are* chosen" (Mt 22:14 NASB). Does it take a great deal of effort to be saved? Is salvation only for the elite performers?

Or consider the story of the rich young ruler who asked Jesus, "What must I do to inherit eternal life?" (Mk 10:17-22//Mt 19:16-22// Lk 18:18-23).[5] Jesus first replied to keep the commandments: "You shall not murder, you shall not commit adultery, you shall not steal, you shall not give false testimony, you shall not defraud, honor your father and mother." That sounds pretty legalistic. But when the man said that he had done this since he was a boy, it got even worse. Jesus added just one little thing: "Go, sell everything you have and give to the poor, and you will have treasure in heaven. Then come, follow me" (Mk 10:21). What? To inherit eternal life you have to keep the commandments *and* sell everything you own? This sounds pretty radical. And it sounds like salvation by works.

Self-mutilation for the Gospel? It gets even worse. Jesus called for radical self-denial and even self-mutilation as a means to avoid the fires of hell:

> If your hand or your foot causes you to stumble, cut it off and throw it away. It is better for you to enter life maimed or crippled than to have two hands or two feet and be thrown

into eternal fire. And if your eye causes you to stumble, gouge
it out and throw it away. It is better for you to enter life with
one eye than to have two eyes and be thrown into the fire of
hell. (Mt 18:8-9//Mk 9:43-48; Mt 5:29-30; Mt 19:12)

Cut off your hand or foot to avoid sin? Gouge out your eye so you
won't lust? Isn't this a little extreme?

So was Jesus a legalist? Did he teach that we earn salvation by
what we do? Did he call for radical self-denial, even to the point of
self-mutilation to prevent sin? Did he warn that hell awaited those
who didn't shape up?

GRACE-FUL PARABLES

Surprisingly, Jesus not only demanded over-the-top high standards
and self-discipline, he also taught that salvation was a free gift from
God. Some of Jesus' most memorable parables highlight God's
grace and free offer of forgiveness.

The parable of the lost son. Perhaps Jesus' most famous and beloved parable is the story of the prodigal son in Luke 15. This parable
takes us to the heart of Jesus' message and the heart of the good news.

In his desire for freedom and independence, a young man makes
a series of very bad decisions. He asks his father to liquidate the
family assets and to give him his share of the inheritance (Lk 15:12).
This seems rude and disrespectful in our culture, but it would be
even more so in the first-century Jewish world. Respect for elders
was a huge value, and parents were to be honored, esteemed and
respected. To ask for your inheritance would be like saying, "Hey,
Dad, I wish you were dead!"

If the son's request is scandalous, the father's response is equally
shocking. It was considered foolish to give inheritance to your
children before your deathbed—especially to an immature son.
One Jewish wisdom book of Jesus' day says it this way:

To son or wife, to brother or friend,
>   do not give power over yourself, as long as you live;
> and do not give your property to another. . . .
> For it is better that your children should ask from you
>   than that you should look to the hand of your children. . . .
> At the time when you end the days of your life,
>   in the hour of death, distribute your inheritance. (Sirach
>   33:20, 22, 24 NRSV)

So already we recognize that there's something very wrong—very countercultural—about this story. What's wrong with this kid? What's wrong with this dad?

At this point, though, the story takes the course most of Jesus' hearers would expect. The immature boy pays the price for his irresponsibility. He wastefully squanders his inheritance partying with his newfound friends. And just as his resources are running thin, the economy turns bad. Jobs are scarce and the only work he can get is feeding pigs. Pigs were considered unclean or defiled animals in Judaism, so this is the worst possible job, a great candidate for the show *Dirty Jobs.* The boy is starving, and even the carob pods that the pigs eat look good.

I remember the worst job I ever had. I was a freshman at San Diego State University and desperate for a job. Every job on campus—even the dreaded fast food—seemed to be taken. Finally, I saw a little 3x5 card on a bulletin board offering $5 per hour for an unspecified service. I called and was chagrined to find it was phone soliciting (I'm a terrible salesperson). I lasted two days, without making a single sale. I still have the cursing of all those little old ladies who hung up on me ringing in my ears.

The boy in our story has finally had enough. An old rabbinic proverb says, "When the Israelites are reduced to carob pods, then they repent."[6] Eating carob pods—pig food—represents pretty much the lowest you can sink. Another Jewish proverb from about this time says, "When a son abroad goes barefoot, then he remembers the comfort of his father's house."[7] "Barefoot" isn't meant to recall the lazy days of summer at the beach. It means so poor you can't even afford shoes.

I remember that first year of college. I moved out of my parent's house and into an apartment with a buddy, thirty miles from home. It was so great to finally have my freedom! The first few weeks were awesome. But then I came to realize that "freedom" meant freedom to pay my own rent, freedom to pay utilities, freedom to eat Kraft macaroni and cheese or Top Ramen five nights a week.

So I started dropping by home now and then (you know, just to pick up stuff I'd forgotten). I'd usually show up around dinner time ("Oh, is it 5:30? I didn't notice. Sure I guess I can stay for dinner, if you insist."). I'd just happen to have my laundry over my shoulder ("Oh, this? I was just on the way to the laundromat. No, I don't want you to do it. Well, okay, if you insist."). For the first time in my life it dawned on me how much my parents had actually done for me—and how little I had appreciated it.

That's what dawns on the boy in Jesus' story. Destitute and starving, he comes to his senses. Even his father's servants have enough food to eat. He makes a decision: he will return to his father and take the role of a hired hand. He practices his speech: "Father, I have sinned against heaven and against you. I am no longer worthy to be called your son; make me like one of your hired servants" (Lk 15:18-19).

At this point Jesus' hearers would be nodding in agreement. The boy is a fool. He needs to admit his error, to come groveling back. He should take a job as a servant and (perhaps) gradually earn his way back into the family.

Yet again the father surprises. As the boy nears home, his father sees him from far away and is overwhelmed with compassion for him. This shows he has been longing and hoping for his return, scanning the horizon every day. He is not the aloof, dispassionate patriarch we would expect. When he sees his son, he *runs* to meet him and embraces him (Lk 15:20). This too is shocking behavior in a Middle Eastern context. The revered patriarch of a family would never run anywhere. Only children and slaves ran. The members of the household would approach the patriarch with honor and respect. The point is that the father doesn't care about dignity. He will play the fool to show his love for his son.

When the boy begins his memorized speech, the father cuts him off (Lk 15:21-22). No time for apologies. He calls his servants to bring the best robe in the house (no doubt the patriarch's own robe), to put a ring on his son's finger (a signet ring indicating authority as a child and heir), and to bring sandals (slaves went barefoot; children destined to be heirs wore shoes). Most shocking of all, he commands that they prepare a great banquet for the boy, killing a calf fattened for slaughter (Lk 15:23). Again we gain insight from Middle Eastern culture. Meat was eaten only on special occasions in Jewish village life. To kill a fattened calf—a large animal!—was something done only for a wedding feast or for a visiting dignitary. This pushes the story to the limits of credibility. Treat a wayward, disrespectful son, who has shamed the entire family with his behavior, as a visiting dignitary? This is absurd. This is scandalous.

But that's exactly the point. This is a story about God's amazing, overwhelming, unmerited grace. The story is traditionally known as the parable of the prodigal son. The word *prodigal* means "wasteful" or "lavish to a fault." But this story is not just about the prodigal *son*; it is also about the prodigal *father*. From the perspective of first-century Jewish culture, the father is shockingly lavish in his love for his son. This is over-the-top grace. This is like rewarding with a raise and a Christmas bonus an executive who has just been caught stealing company funds. It's like giving keys to the Porsche to the son who's been arrested for speeding and reckless driving.

While the father offers unearned and undeserved grace, the older brother responds as one might expect. When he hears there's a party going on for his brother, he is enraged and refuses to join in (Lk 15:25-28). When his father comes out and encourages him to join the celebration, he reminds him that he has "slaved" for his father all these years and has never been given such a party (Lk 15:28-29). He can't even bring himself to refer to his sibling as "my brother," instead calling him "this son of yours." He even makes his brother's behavior sound worse, claiming that he has "squandered your property with prostitutes" (Lk 15:30).

The father again responds with grace, this time directed at the older son: "My son, . . . you are always with me, and everything I have is yours. But we had to celebrate and be glad, because this brother of yours was dead and is alive again; he was lost and is found" (Lk 15:31-32).

This is not just a parable but also an allegory, with each character representing people in Jesus' ministry. The father represents God, who longs for his wayward children to return to him. The younger brother represents the sinners and outcasts with whom Jesus is spending so much time. Though undeserving sinners, they are responding with joy and acceptance to his offer of the kingdom of God. The older brother represents the religious leaders who despise these sinners and criticize Jesus for hanging out with them. They believe they have worked hard to earn their position before God and others must earn it as well.

This parable illustrates that Jesus' message is God's free grace and forgiveness offered to sinners who will repent and return to their Father. Salvation is not something earned by obedience or hard work ("slaving"). It is a free gift from God. This doesn't sound like legalism.

More grace-filled parables. The parable of the prodigal son is not alone. A number of other parables illustrate God's salvation as a free and undeserved gift. In the parable of the great banquet (Lk 14:15-24; cf. Mt 22:2-14), a man has invited a number of guests to a great banquet. This is probably a wedding banquet, lavish affairs that would go on for a week or two. Although the invited guests have long since RSVP'd, when the servants go out to announce that the banquet is ready, the guests all begin to make excuses. One has just bought a field and wants to inspect it; another has just bought some oxen and wants to test them out; a third has just gotten married.

The host can't believe it! He is furious, having invested so much time and money in this event. But instead of lashing out at those who have snubbed him, he widens the invitation to people on the fringes of society: the poor, the crippled, the blind and the lame.

While to our ears this might sound like just a nice bit of charity work, it would have been shocking to first-century ears. Dinner parties like this in the ancient Mediterranean world were rituals of social status. You held a banquet to raise your position in the community. You would invite people of higher status so that they would honor you by inviting you back. This is a culture of *reciprocity*, where you would give in order to get. Think of it like a time-share presentation today. You're invited to a nice steak dinner with all the trimmings and then you have to sit through a high pressure sales pitch in hopes that you will invest in their properties. (My wife hates these things and refuses to go. I love steak and lobster, and so am easily seduced.)

What is shocking about this parable is that *nobody* in that culture would turn around and invite people who have no status—the poor, crippled, blind and lame—to such a banquet, since these people could give nothing in return. (See Jesus' radical teaching just before this in Luke 14:12-14, where he says you should invite such people to your parties precisely because they can't pay you back.) In the context of Jesus' ministry, the parable is about Jesus' announcement of the kingdom of God, viewed as an invitation to a banquet. The invited guests represent the religious leaders of Israel, who are snubbing Jesus' call to repentance and faith. Jesus turns instead to the outcasts in Israel—the poor, the handicapped, sinners, tax collectors, prostitutes and other riffraff who joyfully accept his invitation. They have nothing to offer in return, but the invitation to the party has no strings attached. Salvation is a free gift, not something earned by work.

Other parables also illustrate God's free grace. In the parable of the workers in the vineyard (Mt 20:1-16), a vineyard owner hires a succession of laborers to work his vineyard, some early in the morning, others at 9:00 a.m., others at noon, and still others at 3:00 p.m. But at the end of the day, he pays them all the same, one denarius, which is a standard day's wage. When those who have worked longer object, the owner says essentially, "Can't I do whatever I want with my own money? Why are you bothered that I'm being generous?" The parable at first sight seems puzzling and unjust. Shouldn't greater work receive greater pay? Yet Jesus' point is that *everything* we receive is a gift from God. The "reward" is not based on the amount of work performed, but on the generosity of the owner. This is a parable about God's grace. As R. T. France points out,

> Anyone who took this parable as a practical basis for employment would soon be out of business. But the kingdom of heaven does not operate on the basis of commercial convention. God rules by grace, not by desert. . . . The God who lavishly clothes the flowers and feeds the birds delights to give his servants far more than they could ever deserve from him.[8]

RESOLVING THE PARADOX: RADICAL KINGDOM COMMITMENT AND SPIRIT-EMPOWERED OBEDIENCE

So was Jesus a legalist, demanding obedience to a list of rules and commandments? Or was he offering salvation as a free gift to anyone who asked? Answers can be found by examining Jesus' teaching on the nature of salvation in the kingdom of God.

Camels and needles' eyes: Salvation through the power of God. One of the most difficult passages in the Gospels is the story of the rich young ruler (Mk 10:17-31//Mt 19:16-30//Lk 18:18-30). First, Jesus tells the man that to inherit eternal life he must keep the Ten Commandments. This seems like salvation by works. Then, when the man claims to have faithfully kept them, Jesus sets the bar extraordinarily high by telling him he must sell everything he has and give the proceeds to the poor. Finally, he confounds the disciples by asserting that, "It is easier for a camel to go through the eye of a needle than for someone who is rich to enter the kingdom of God" (Mk 10:25).

The keys to this passage are Jesus' statements at the beginning and the end. When the man first addresses Jesus as "good teacher," Jesus challenges his notion of goodness: "Why do you call me good? . . . No one is good—except God" (Mk 10:17). Jesus is not denying that he is God, as some have supposed. The man has no conception that Jesus is God, so such a point would be meaningless. Jesus is rather picking up on the man's language to make a rhetorical point. The man thinks Jesus is a good teacher. Jesus responds that in comparison to God's perfection, *no human being is good.* Even before the man claims to have faithfully kept all the commandments (Mk 10:20), Jesus nullifies his claim! No one is good except God.

At the end of the episode, then, when Jesus uses the extreme hyperbole of a camel trying to get through the eye of the needle, the disciples ask incredulously, "Who then can be saved?" (Mk 10:26). Riches were generally viewed in Judaism as a sign of God's blessing, especially for those who demonstrated piety in their lives.[9] If this pious rich man who has faithfully kept the Ten Commandments cannot be saved, then who can be? The answer is no one. No one but God is good, and so no one can be saved *while trusting in their own riches, goodness or abilities.* That camel will never ever get through the eye of a needle! You could slice, dice and chop it, or put it in a blender and try to shoot it through. But there is still no way that camel will make it through. It is impossible.

Throughout history people have tried to soften Jesus' words. One interpretation is that there was a small gate leading into Jerusalem known as the "Needle's-Eye Gate." A camel could pass through it only by having its baggage removed and crawling on its belly. In this case Jesus would be teaching that rich people can enter the kingdom only by unburdening themselves of their love for riches. The problem with this interpretation is that it is simply wrong. There never was a gate by this name in Jerusalem in the first century. This interpretation is first attested in the eleventh century in a commentary by Theophylact of Bulgaria, a thousand years after Christ![10]

To understand Jesus' words, we need to listen to what he actually says. The climax of his teaching is that "with man this is impossible, but not with God; all things are possible with God" (Mk 10:27). It is *impossible* for a rich person, or any person, to enter the kingdom of God through human effort. It is only by God's power and grace that people are saved. The rich man is trusting in his riches instead of in God and so fails.

Passages like this can make us—especially those who live in the prosperous Western world—very uncomfortable. Was Jesus a socialist, telling people to give up their wealth for the common good? Was he a radical, calling for the repudiation of all possessions? We usually explain away this passage by saying, "Wealth was *this guy's* problem, so Jesus told *him* he needed to give it up. He didn't tell us to do the same." Then we breathe a sigh of relief.

But sighers beware. Anyone who is relieved by assuming the command is only for this man is missing the point. Salvation costs us nothing; it is a free gift from God. But it costs us everything, giving up our lives and receiving God's life. Jesus said that those who want to be his disciples must *deny themselves, take up their cross and follow him* (Mk 8:34//Mt 16:24//Lk 9:23). To take up your cross means to die—to die to yourself and live for God. Our life is no longer our own. It is God's.

When Jesus began preaching the kingdom, his message was "Repent and believe the good news!" (Mk 1:15). *Repent* means to turn away from sin and to reorient one's life to God. *Believe* means to trust in God alone for salvation. That is the opposite of salvation by works. It is salvation through dependence on God—faith alone. Yet it is also a radical call to discipleship, a demand to give up *all* to follow him. In Romans 6:22 Paul says, "Now that you have been set free from sin and have become slaves of God, the benefit you reap leads to holiness, and the result is eternal life."

What about eye gouging and hand chopping? Jesus' apparent calls for self-mutilation to prevent sin (Mt 5:29-30; 18:8-9//Mk 9:43-48; Mt 19:12) must also be understood in the context of radical commitment to the kingdom. What is the kingdom of God worth? What should we give up to inherit it? The simply answer is everything.

In Matthew 13:45-46 Jesus compares the kingdom of God to a merchant who discovers a beautiful pearl. He likes it so much he sells everything he has to buy it. On the face of it the parable is absurd. Suppose on our anniversary I presented my wife with a beautiful pearl necklace. She responds, "It's beautiful, but can we afford it?" "Well," I say, "I had to sell the house to buy it." "What!" she says, "The house—what were you thinking?" "No problem, we can live on the street. Oh, and I had to sell our cars and empty out our bank accounts. And I cashed in our retirement." "What?" she says. Then she looks around, "Wait a minute, where are the kids?"

Do you see how absurd this is? Who would sell *everything* they own for a pearl? But the pearl represents the kingdom of God, and the kingdom represents the restoration of creation and a relationship with the creator God. What is that worth? It is worth everything.

Jesus is not telling people they should start gouging out their eyes and chopping off their hands every time they have a lustful thought. He is instead making a powerful rhetorical point meant to shock his readers. He is announcing the kingdom of God, the climax of human history. It is time to make a radical commitment and get onboard. It will cost you nothing; it is solely by faith. But it will cost you everything—your whole life.

Being perfect, as your heavenly Father is perfect (Mt 5:48). If Jesus taught that we were saved by faith alone, how do we explain his command to "be perfect, . . . as your heavenly Father is perfect" (Mt 5:48)? The answer must be found in the radical transformation of the law that comes with the kingdom of God.

Jesus said that he did not come to abolish the law, but to *fulfill it* (Mt 5:17). He fulfilled the law in two ways. First, he lived a life of perfect obedience and so fulfilled the requirements of the law. Second, he brought the law to its intended culmination, by paying the penalty for our sins through his sacrificial death on the cross. Paul writes, "Christ is the culmination of the law so that there may be righteousness for everyone who believes" (Rom 10:4).

The author of Hebrews discusses Jesus' role as the fulfillment of the law. The Old Testament law was incapable of bringing salvation. It could only point out our sin. "The law is only a shadow of the good things that are coming—not the realities themselves. For this reason it can never, by the same sacrifices repeated endlessly year after year, make perfect those who draw near to worship" (Heb 10:1). Yet what the law could not do, Jesus did through his sacrificial death on the cross: "For by one sacrifice he has made perfect forever those who are being made holy" (Heb 10:14). Believers become "perfect" not by legalistically outperforming others but by receiving Christ's perfection through faith. We receive his life by identifying with him in his life, death and resurrection. Paul says, "I have been crucified with Christ and I no longer live, but Christ lives in me. The life I now live in the body, I live by faith in the Son of God, who loved me and gave himself for me" (Gal 2:20).

What about the passages about the great difficulty of entering heaven or inheriting eternal life? It is important to examine each of these in context. In Luke 13:23-30, after calling his followers to strive or "make every effort" to enter the narrow door to the kingdom, Jesus provides an analogy of the owner of a house who closes the door after letting some in. When others knock on the door, he replies, "I don't know you or where you come from" (Lk 13:25). Notice that entrance into the banquet is not something that is earned. The host doesn't ask if the guests have paid their entrance fees. It is about *knowing Christ*—a relationship with him. The parable ends with people from all parts of the globe coming to the feast in the kingdom of God, but the elite within Israel being left out. Obedience to the law or physical ancestry does not bring salvation. It is received by knowing Jesus, who through his life, death and resurrection has fulfilled the law and inaugurated the kingdom of God.

The same point is made in Matthew 22:14 ("Many are called, but few are chosen" [ESV]), which occurs at the end of Matthew's parable of the wedding banquet (Mt 22:1-14). The first phrase would be better translated, "Many are *invited* . . ." (NIV), since it refers to those in the parable who have been invited to the banquet (i.e., the kingdom of God). While Jesus' invitation to the kingdom is going out to all, only a few are responding positively to the invitation and receiving its salvation benefits.

Righteousness that surpasses that of the Pharisees and the scribes (Mt 5:20). So how can the righteousness of Jesus' followers surpass that of the Pharisees and scribes, who meticulously kept the law (Mt 5:20)? Again the answer must be found in the power and presence of the kingdom of God.

Jesus said that in his own words and actions, God's kingdom was breaking into human history. To understand the implications of this for the law of Moses we must examine the Old Testament background. While Israel repeatedly broke God's commandments and failed to keep his covenant, God remained faithful. In Jeremiah 31 he promised that a time of salvation was coming (i.e., the kingdom of God), when God would establish a *new covenant* with his people. This new covenant would provide eternal forgiveness of sins, intimate knowledge of God and *the law written on their hearts* (Jer 31:31-34; cf. Heb 8:6-13; Lk 22:20; 1 Cor 11:25).

How can the law be written on human hearts? The answer is that the new age of salvation is the age of the Spirit of God. Repeatedly in the Old Testament, God promised that when his end-time salvation came, he would pour out his Spirit to fill, guide and empower his people. Ezekiel 36:26-27 reads, "I will give you a new heart and put a new spirit in you; I will remove from you your heart of stone and give you a heart of flesh. And I will put my Spirit in you and move you to follow my decrees and be careful to keep my laws" (see also Is 44:3; Joel 2:28; Acts 2). We see here how our righteousness can exceed that of the scribes and Pharisees. As people of the kingdom, we have something they did not have—the Spirit of God living in us. The Holy Spirit provides believers with the power and presence of God to fulfill the law.

This also explains why Jesus raises the bar in the Sermon on the Mount. He says that anger is equivalent to murder and that lust is equivalent to adultery (Mt 5:21-30). He is pushing beyond mere human effort to a true heart obedience arising from the internal transformation—the new heart—provided by the Holy Spirit. Jesus' followers live to a higher standard because they have a greater resource, the Spirit of God living in them.

The apostle Paul speaks a great deal about the Spirit's empowering presence in the new age of salvation. Anyone who is "in Christ" is part of the new creation (2 Cor 5:17), and as part of the new creation they have received God's Spirit, enabling them to live a life of spiritual victory and obedience to God's commands (Rom 8:1-17).

Transformation resulting in obedience. A distinction must therefore be made here between *entrance* into the kingdom of God—a free gift offered to sinners—and the righteousness that comes from a life transformed by the power and presence of the Spirit of God. Those who become children of God through faith enter the kingdom of God and so receive the Spirit of God, which provides the power and the potential to live a new life.

This resolution helps to explain other paradoxes between New Testament authors. While Paul insists that we are saved by God's grace alone, not by our works (Eph 2:8-9), James claims that faith without works is useless and dead (Jas 2:14-26). There is no contradiction here. Paul is referring to the means by which we come into a relationship with God and asserts that Christ's death alone pays for our sins. James is speaking about the life of obedience that results from this transformation.

Just as an adopted child does nothing to earn entrance into a family, so we can do nothing to earn our status as God's children. We receive it as a free gift. Yet, once the adoption takes place, we have a responsibility to live as obedient children and to share that love with others. The privilege comes with responsibility. Not only that, but we have been given the power to do so because the gift of salvation comes with the empowering presence of the Spirit of God—Christ in you, the hope of glory.

Conclusion

Years ago I worked for an alcoholism counseling agency. I was a psychology major in college and this was my internship. As part of my responsibilities I did some counseling and also taught drunk-driving courses. No, I didn't teach people to drive drunk. These were court-ordered classes for those who had received a first DUI. In class we talked about the dangers of driving intoxicated and how to find your appropriate limits.

The first day of class I would go around the room and let my students vent, describing how they ended up in this situation. It was amazing how few were actually guilty! It was almost always a corrupt officer, a false positive on the Breathalyzer or an irresponsible judge. I learned a lot about the human capacity for self-justification. I also became quite a crusader against drunk driving and the destruction it wreaks in people's lives.

One night after teaching my course I was driving home and stopped at a little grocery store to pick up some items. The old guy in front of me in the checkout line was obviously intoxicated. He was purchasing two big bottles of vodka and was making small talk and cracking jokes with the pretty clerk. As I listened I began to despise the guy. I imagined him getting into his car and driving away, hitting some poor child. I hated him and all he stood for.

He left, and I paid for my items. But as I got into my car and pulled into the street, I saw him again. He wasn't driving; he was walking slowly down the street. He had that awkward shuffling gate of a long-term alcoholic. I watched him for a moment and suddenly saw him differently. I imagined him walking alone back to his empty little apartment, drinking himself into oblivion, getting up the next day and doing it again. My heart of hatred melted, and for first time I saw him as God did, as a prodigal whose Father longed to have him home.

This man slowly shuffling down the road was no different from me or you. He was just a sinner trapped in his sin, desperately in need of God's grace. Salvation is receiving the gift of forgiveness and grace that comes from God. Then it is the grateful response that comes from this—the desire to share the gift with others.

But God demonstrates his own love for us in this: While we were still sinners, Christ died for us. (Rom 5:8)

Dear friends, since God so loved us, we also ought to love one another. (1 Jn 4:11)

HELLFIRE PREACHER
OR GENTLE SHEPHERD?

SCARING THE HELL OUT OF YOU

THEY CALL THEM "HELL HOUSES." Inspired by traditional haunted houses, these attractions pop up around the country during Halloween season, usually operated by conservative Christian groups and churches. One the most famous is operated by Trinity Church in Cedar Hill, Texas, now in its twenty-fourth year. The church's planning and implementation of the event was the topic of a 2001 documentary *Hell House*.

The purpose of a Hell House is, quite literally, to scare the hell out of you. Participants purchase a ticket and then walk through a variety of scenes depicting the horrific consequences of sin. One room might show a late-term abortion that has been botched, a bloody fetus lies on the table beside a distressed and screaming girl. She is covered with blood and baby parts. A doctor and several nurses stand by, sneering with detached and uncaring cynicism. The next room portrays a dark-hooded crowd practicing a Satanic ritual. A pentagram is scratched in a table and a baby is about to be killed in a human sacrifice. Moving on you come to a darkened room where demons dance around an overdose victim. The corpse's eyes are rolled back and a heroin needle dangles from his limp arm. The cackling demons dance with delight at the prospect of tormenting their victim for eternity. The final scenes in a Hell House usually contrast the horrors of hell with the eternal joys of heaven. Flyers are distributed with verses from the Bible and the plan of salvation explained.

Though these macabre venues are quite popular around Halloween, I think most Christians cringe at the thought of coaxing people to follow Jesus by scaring the bejeebers out of them. Indeed, hell is one of the most difficult and controversial doctrines of the Christian faith. It is also one of the most uncomfortable. Some people I've talked to claim they cannot believe in Christianity because of this teaching.

Many think of hell as an Old Testament idea. One online reviewer of the documentary *Hell House* says, "This is old style 'fire and brimstone' scare tactics straight out of the Old Testament." After all, the God of the Old Testament seems to many to be an angry old man, wiping out the world with a massive flood, raining fire and brimstone down on Sodom and Gomorrah, opening up the earth and swallowing whole families.

But in fact the idea of eternal damnation is barely mentioned in the Old Testament (only really in Daniel 12:2 and perhaps Isaiah 66:24). Others might turn next to the apostle Paul. After all, Paul seems to be a pretty stern and judgmental guy, warning about the wages of sin and the wrath of God. But in fact, there is barely a singe of hell in Paul's writings.[1]

JESUS AS HELLFIRE PREACHER?

Surprisingly, the person who talked about hell the most in the Bible was Jesus! That's right, the same guy who said to love your enemies and forgive those who wrong you seven times seventy also talked a lot about the red-hot fires that awaited the enemies of God. The same guy who welcomed little children and showed compassion for the poor and sick described hell as a place where "the worms . . . do not die, and the fire is not quenched" (Mk 9:48).

What is hell? A cartoon on my office door at work shows a husband and wife entering a department store. In front of them are two escalators, one going up and the other down. The first has a sign reading "Hardware," and the second "Ladies' Shoes." The man sees the signs in his mind as "Heaven" and "Hell," respectively. I can relate. We sometimes refer to hell as things we find particularly distasteful or obnoxious. Yet the Bible takes a more serious perspective, describing hell as a place of ultimate judgment and justice.

The word most commonly translated "hell" in the New Testament comes from the Hebrew term *Gehenna*, meaning the "valley of (the son of) Hinnom." This was the valley on the southwestern side of Jerusalem that became notorious as a place of pagan sacrifices, where children were burned alive as an offering to the Canaanite gods Molech and Baal (2 Chron 28:3; 33:6; Jer 7:31; 19:5-6; 32:35). King Josiah destroyed the shrines in the valley to stop this pagan practice (2 Kings 23:10), and the place came to be used for dumping and burning garbage. In the period between the Old and New Testaments, the name *Gehenna* began to be used symbolically for the place of divine punishment—the fires of hell.[2]

Another word, *Hades*, is Greek in origin. In Greek thought it referred to the underworld or the place of the dead. The word is used in various ways in the New Testament, usually meaning simply "the place of the dead" or "the grave." Occasionally it refers to a place of torment. Jesus warns the town of Capernaum that it will go down to Hades because it rejected the works of the Messiah (Mt 11:23; Lk 10:15), and in the parable of the rich man and Lazarus, the rich man after death finds himself in torment in Hades (Lk 16:23).[3] Jesus tells Peter that the "gates of Hades" will not be able to withstand the advance of his church (Mt 16:18). At the end of the book of Revelation, death and Hades are thrown into the lake of fire, which is referred to as "the second death" (Rev 20:13-15; cf. Rev 19:20; 20:10). The lake of fire (or burning sulfur) appears to be synonymous with Gehenna or hell.

Jesus' teaching on hell (Gehenna). Although Jesus never opened a Hell House or condoned one, we have to acknowledge that he did talk quite a bit about hell. Jesus taught that if you call someone a fool, you are in danger of the fires of hell (Mt 5:22). He said that people should not fear those who can kill the body, but instead should fear God, who can throw them into hell (Mt 10:28//Lk 12:5). On another occasion Jesus encouraged his followers to mutilate themselves by cutting off their hands or plucking out their eyes rather than to sin with these body parts and so risk hellfire (Mt 5:29-30//Mk 9:43-48; Mt 18:8-9). He warned the religious leaders that their hypocritical actions would result in condemnation to hell (Mt 23:33).

Jesus also refers to hell in a number of parables. The parable of the tares and the parable of the nets, both of which speak of the separation of the righteous and the wicked, refer to those who will be thrown into "the blazing furnace, where there will be weeping and gnashing of teeth" (Mt 13:42, 50). In the parable of the wedding feast, a man cast out of the banquet is thrown "outside, into the darkness, where there will be weeping and gnashing of teeth" (Mt 22:13; cf. Mt 8:10-12//Lk 13:28; Mt 24:51). The same phrase is used in the parable of the talents, where the "worthless servant" is similarly cast out (Mt 25:30). In the parable of the sheep and the goats, Jesus tells those he condemns, "Depart from me, you who are cursed, into the eternal fire prepared for the devil and his angels" (Mt 25:41). Finally, as noted earlier, in the parable of the rich man and Lazarus, the rich man finds himself in torment in Hades (Lk 16:23).

This is a heck of a lot of hell. How do we account for Jesus' apparent obsession with the punishment of the wicked in the afterlife? Where is the Jesus of love, forgiveness and compassion?

RESOLVING THE PARADOX: GOD'S LOVE AND JUSTICE

There is little doubt that Jesus believed in hell. And he expected certain people to go there. In his teaching, hell is a place of torment, weeping and gnashing of teeth. Though it was originally prepared for the devil and his angels, people too find their destiny there.

Is a doctrine like this cruel and vindictive—inappropriate for a wise and compassionate teacher like Jesus? Some think that these sayings must have been put into the mouth of Jesus by the later church, since this peace-loving teacher would never have said such things. Yet this seems unlikely. There are too many sayings attributed to Jesus on hell for this teaching to have been created whole cloth by the church.

A better solution is to recognize that the doctrine of divine judgment is not a primitive or vengeful teaching. It is an *essential consequence of the character of a God*, who is both loving and just.

The world's history of evil and injustice. The history of the world is in many respects a history of evil and injustice. Many crimes go unsolved, with murderers never caught. An Internet search reveals a long list of unsolved serial killings, from Jack the Ripper in nineteenth-century London to the "Alphabet Murders" in the early 1970s around Rochester, New York (whose victims' first and last names all started with the same letter of the alphabet) to the "Highway of Tears" murders, a 900-mile stretch of Highway 16 in Canada, where over forty young women have disappeared. Or consider Ciudad Juaréz, sometimes called the City of Lost Girls, a poor Mexican border town where hundreds (some claim thousands) of women have been raped, tortured and killed over the past decades. Most of the women are poor, working in the numerous factories located close to the US–Mexican border. Partly because of the drug wars raging in the region, few assailants are ever caught or tried.[4] There is little justice here.

These are just a few examples of thousands of unsolved murders each year, where assailants were never caught or were arrested and set free because of lack of evidence, or were able to bribe their way through corrupt court systems. History shows that justice is often not served.

Even when perpetrators are caught and tried, there seems to be little justice. Dennis Rader, the BTK killer (for "bind, torture, kill"— his method), tortured and then murdered ten people in Sedgwick County, Kansas, between 1974 and 1991. He is serving ten consecutive life sentences in prison, eating three square meals a day. Jeffrey Dahmer murdered at least seventeen men and boys between 1978 and 1991. His murders were particularly gruesome, involving acts of forced necrophilia, dismemberment and cannibalism. Dahmer was eventually beaten to death in prison, after receiving fifteen consecutive life terms. Many names could be added: Ted Bundy, John Wayne Gacy, David Berkowitz—all serial killers who were eventually caught, tried and either executed or sentenced to life in prison. But is this justice? The punishment seems small in comparison to the terrible nature of their crime.

Then there is the long list of genocidal atrocities around the world: the Nazi Holocaust during World War II, where over six million Jews were murdered in gas chambers and other forms of execution; the killing fields of Cambodia during the 1970s, where Pol Pot and his Khmer Rouge murdered over a million victims; the tribal genocide of Rwanda over a period of one hundred days between April and July 1994, where almost a million Rwandans, mostly Tutsis and moderate Hutus, were massacred by radical Hutu rivals. Men, women and children were brutally murdered, most hacked to death with machetes. Then there was the "ethnic cleansing" in Bosnia and Herzegovina during the Bosnian War of the 1990s, when tens of thousands of Bosnian Muslims and Croats were murdered, raped, tortured, beaten and subjected to inhumane treatment. While some of the perpetrators of these crimes were eventually arrested, tried and convicted, most escaped punishment.

These atrocities, of course, were all from the past century, the most "civilized" era of human history. Consider the countless millions who have been exploited, oppressed, tortured and killed throughout human history. Occasionally, justice is served. But just as often, evil is left unpunished. The wicked prosper and the innocent perish. History is in many ways a depressing chronicle of evil people committing evil acts.

Hell as the promise and reality of God's justice. Now imagine a world where evil is never punished, where atrocities like these are the end of the story. The biblical teaching on hell is directly linked to the doctrine of divine justice. It is the message that, though evil appears to go unpunished in this world, there is an all-knowing, all-powerful Judge who keeps perfect records, and who will one day justly judge all the evil of this world.

When seen in this light, hell is not a fiery torture chamber cooked up in the imagination of angry medieval clerics. It is the *necessity* of a just and righteous God, who hears the cries of the poor, oppressed and exploited.

Jesus' teaching about hell is an affirmation of the justice of God. If God is just and righteous, then sin must be punished and wrong must be made right. If perpetrators of evil are not made to pay for their crimes, then there is no justice in the world—and so, no God worthy of our worship.

THE NATURE OF HELL

While the reality of hell is an essential doctrine for maintaining the justice of God, its nature is greatly debated. Many theologians object to the nature and extent of hell rather than to its reality. Even among Christians who consider the Bible to be the divinely inspired Word of God, there are various views of hell. Here are three.

Eternal, conscious torment. The traditional view is that hell involves the eternal, conscious torment of the unrighteous in a place separated from God.[5] The primary images related to hell are fire and darkness. Jesus spoke of the "fire of hell" (Mt 5:22; 18:9), a "blazing furnace" (Mt 13:42, 50), "eternal fire" (Mt 25:41) and a place of "darkness" (Mt 8:12; 22:13; 25:29). The fire here may be metaphorical, since fire and darkness would normally be incompatible. Of course metaphorical does not mean unreal, but only that the suffering is being described in ways that are comprehensible to us. Whether metaphorical or literal, the fire and darkness clearly involve extreme torment and suffering.

Hell is also a place of great sorrow. People there weep and gnash their teeth (Mt 8:12; 13:42, 50; 22:13; 25:30). Weeping is a symbol of sorrow and suffering. Gnashing is a sign of extreme frustration and turmoil. Hell's duration is forever. It is an "eternal fire" (Mt 25:41) and a place where "THEIR WORM DOES NOT DIE, AND THE FIRE IS NOT QUENCHED" (Mk 9:48 NASB; alluding to Is 66:24).

The strongest objection to this portrayal of hell is the apparent injustice involved. Why would God punish *temporal* sins with *eternal* consequences? Shouldn't the punishment fit the crime? Put another way, justice should be just, so people receive punishment equivalent to their evil. Even the worst offender's crimes are limited, not infinite. One might say that Hitler should suffer the penalty equivalent to ten million horrific deaths for his terrible crimes against humanity. But ten million is far less than *eternal,* unrelenting suffering.

A common response to this argument is that *all sin* is an offense against an *infinitely holy and perfect God.* By its very nature sin incurs an infinite penalty. All sin should justly receive eternal separation from God in hell.

For those who still find eternal, conscious torment to be incompatible with the justice of God, two main alternatives have been proposed. Both involve limited punishment. The first, universal or ultimate reconciliation, claims that ultimately and eventually all people will be saved. The second claims that the torment of hell is limited and that the souls of the wicked will cease to exist after appropriate punishment.

Universalism or ultimate reconciliation. There are many versions of universalism. Some claim that God simply accepts all people into his presence; others that all religions lead to God; still others that all people will eventually find God in their own way. Since the Bible clearly states that Jesus is the only way to God (Jn 14:6; 1 Tim 2:5; 1 Jn 5:12), the only universalism we will consider here is the view that all people will ultimately be saved *through Christ.* This view is often called *ultimate reconciliation,* since it claims that all people will eventually be reconciled to God through his son Jesus Christ.[6] Since many die without believing in Christ, this version of universalism requires that people have some opportunity after death to respond and believe.

Biblical support for this view is said to come from passages that speak of all people experiencing God's salvation. Consider these statements:

> And I, when I am lifted up from the earth, will draw all people to myself. (Jn 12:32)

> Just as one trespass resulted in condemnation for all people, so also one righteous act resulted in justification and life for all people. (Rom 5:18)

> God has bound everyone over to disobedience so that he may have mercy on them all. (Rom 11:32)

> For as in Adam all die, so in Christ all will be made alive. (1 Cor 15:22)

> At the name of Jesus every knee should bow,
>   in heaven and on earth and under the earth,

and every tongue acknowledge that Jesus Christ is Lord,
    to the glory of God the Father. (Phil 2:10-11)

For the grace of God has been revealed, bringing salvation
    to all people. (Tit 2:11 NLT)

There are also many passages that claim God's salvation has brought, or will bring, ultimate reconciliation between God and his creation. Second Corinthians 5:19 reads, "God was reconciling the world to himself in Christ, not counting people's sins against them." Similarly, Colossians 1:19-20 says that "God was pleased to have all his fullness dwell in him [Christ], and through him to reconcile to himself all things, whether things on earth or things in heaven" (cf. Acts 3:21). If God's reconciliation in Christ concerns "all things . . . on earth or in heaven," how could hell remain burning forever with unreconciled souls in some corner of the universe?

Consider also 1 Timothy 2:3-4, which says that God "wants all people to be saved and to come to a knowledge of the truth." The argument is often made that God always gets what he wants, and so, if he desires all people to be saved, they will surely be saved. A similar statement is made in 2 Peter 3:9: "The Lord . . . is patient with you, not wanting anyone to perish, but everyone to come to repentance." If God desires all people to be saved, who can thwart his will?

Yet there are also significant problems with universalism. First, nowhere in the Bible is there any hint that people can be saved after death. Passages like Hebrews 9:27 would seem to deny this: "people are destined to die once, and after that to face judgment."

Second, in context the statements that "all" will be saved are qualified to refer to all those who respond in faith. The death of one man (Christ) reversed the sin of the one man Adam and made salvation *available to all*, not necessarily received by all. Though God desires all people to be saved, not everyone will respond and receive the gift of salvation. The restoration of creation as a whole does not necessarily mean that every individual within creation will be saved.

Critics of universalism also point out that it trivializes the significance of the death of Christ. If everyone will be saved, then Christ's death is of no value. This argument, however, does not really apply to *Christian* universalism, which claims that everyone will be saved *through the death of Christ*. Critics also point out that universalism eliminates any motivation for evangelism. This too is not quite right, if all will be saved *after a period of judgment and punishment*. Motivation for evangelism could be to call people to avoid the wrath and judgment of God, even if this judgment is limited instead of eternal. Further motivation, of course, is to encourage hurting people to embrace and enjoy the salvation that is available in Christ even now.

Yet when we add to these arguments the many passages in Scripture that speak of the condemnation and destruction of the wicked, universalism does not seem tenable. John 3:36, for example, reads, "Whoever believes in the Son has eternal life, but whoever rejects the Son will not see life, for God's wrath remains on them." "Will not see life" and "God's wrath remains" do not seem to envision ultimate reconciliation. Dozens of similar passages could be cited. Consider this small sampling:

> All who sin apart from the law will also perish apart from the law, and all who sin under the law will be judged by the law. (Rom 2:12)

> Do you not know that wrongdoers will not inherit the kingdom of God? (1 Cor 6:9)

> Do not be deceived: God cannot be mocked. A man reaps what he sows. Whoever sows to please their flesh, from the

flesh will reap destruction; whoever sows to please the Spirit, from the Spirit will reap eternal life. (Gal 6:7-8)

If we deliberately keep on sinning after we have received the knowledge of the truth, no sacrifice for sins is left, but only a fearful expectation of judgment and of raging fire that will consume the enemies of God. (Heb 10:26-27)[7]

These objections are significant, leading some to suggest that hell should be defined neither as eternal, conscious torment nor ultimate reconciliation, but as complete destruction or annihilation.

Annihilationism or conditional immortality. Annihilationism is sometimes called "conditional immortality."[8] The argument is made that since God alone gives life, people's souls are not by nature immortal. Immortality or eternal life is a perpetual gift from God. For the wicked, to be separated from God means to be separated from life and so to experience destruction or annihilation. According to most evangelical annihilationists, the wicked will experience an appropriate and limited period of punishment, after which they will cease to exist.

One strength of annihilationism is that it would seem to preserve the justice of God. Punishment of limited duration is fair compensation for finite sins. People who reject Christ would be judged according to their sins (Rom 2:6). (As noted previously, those who argue for eternal, conscious torment counter that any sin against an *infinite* God merits infinite punishment.)

Annihilationism is also supported by the many passages about final judgment that use the language of "destruction" or "perish" or "consume." Indeed, most passages about judgment use this kind of language (see those listed earlier). John Stott, for decades an evangelical senior statesmen (and an annihilationist), wrote, "It would seem strange, therefore, if people who are said to suffer destruction are in fact not destroyed; . . . it is difficult to imagine a perpetually inconclusive process of perishing."[9] The metaphor of fire would also suit an annihilationist perspective, since fire typically consumes and destroys.

The strongest arguments against annihilationism are those passages that seem to refer to an ongoing torment that lasts forever. Most explicit is Revelation 20:10, which says that the devil, the beast and the false prophet will be thrown into the lake of fire, where "they will be tormented day and night for ever and ever." Jesus' statement that "'the worms that eat them do not die, and the fire is not quenched'" (Mk 9:48; citing Is 66:24) would also seem to indicate ongoing torment. Against this, annihilationists assert that the punishment *is eternal*, since the destruction continues for all eternity. To be annihilated means to be separated from God forever.

CONCLUSION

The question of hell is one of the most difficult and challenging topics in Christian theology. I certainly don't believe we have resolved it in this brief chapter. My purpose has not been to come down in full support of one view of hell over another. The goal has been rather to engage the question of whether Jesus' teaching on hell is vindictive, primitive and unsuitable for a good and loving teacher.

I have sought to show that the doctrine of divine justice (i.e., hell) is not only biblical, it is an essential reality to defend the goodness, justice and righteousness of God. If God did not respond to evil with justice, he would not be a just and loving God.

Of course the transforming power of the gospel is that God *has* judged evil through his Son Jesus Christ, who paid the penalty for our sins. God now offers forgiveness and transformation to all who will accept this free gift of salvation. He is a good and loving and forgiving God.

Yet the reality is that many still refuse to accept this good news. Exactly *how* God will establish his perfect justice for those who reject his salvation remains a difficult question, and one that is not easily resolved on this side of eternity. But that's because God is God and we are not.

> "For my thoughts are not your thoughts,
>   neither are your ways my ways,"
>   declares the LORD.
> "As the heavens are higher than the earth,
>   so are my ways higher than your ways
>   and my thoughts than your thoughts." (Is 55:8-9)

Antifamily or Family Friendly?

Who's Your Daddy?

Karen first met the group that would become her second family during a visit to Seattle. It was the heyday of the Jesus movement in the 1970s. Karen had made a commitment to Jesus Christ earlier, but she was looking for something deeper and more meaningful in her Christian life. So many of the "Jesus People" seemed corny and superficial.

She had heard about a group known as the Love Family and decided to visit. The moment she arrived at the Bible study she felt right at home. Five or six people were gathered in a room talking. They were friendly and polite and talked about Jesus Christ and about being one family based on love. One of the elders of the group encouraged her to read their charter, which was a statement of their beliefs. It was full of all kinds of stuff from the New Testament and the teaching of Jesus. She learned that "the Love Family is a real family, based on love and truth, based on God and Jesus Christ." From the beginning Karen felt she had finally found people who practiced authentic Christianity.

At the time Karen joined, the group had about sixty people, living in seven houses. The founder of the group called himself Love Israel. He was formerly known as Paul Erdman, a one-time salesman who had come to Seattle from California. Love Israel exercised almost total control over his followers. They considered him to be Christ's representative, whose purpose was to gather together God's true family. The members of the group were given new names, representing virtues like Meekness, Integrity, Happiness, Courage and Patience. These were considered their true names, which were eternal gifts from God.

Karen was attracted to the simple, loving and well-ordered life of the group. They did everything together. They got up at the same time, ate together, worked together and worshiped together. This was simple and authentic Christianity!

Members of the group were also encouraged to cut ties with their former family. Karen writes:

> We were urged to cut off all communications with our parents. We were told that we shouldn't write to our parents, because when you are in Jesus Christ, you are starting a new life and the people of our past would hold us back. We had to give up all worldly ties, and our parents were tied with the world. . . . I referred to my biological parents as my "worldly parents" or my "natural parents," but Love Israel didn't really like us to use the word parents at all. He wanted us to refer to them as simply "Jane" and "John" . . . They were not my "real" parents.[1]

The Love Family is just one of thousands of cults and new religious movements in the United States and around the world.[2] Though similar groups have appeared throughout history, the Jesus movement of the 1960s and 1970s saw a great proliferation of them. Most groups like this are led by a strong and charismatic leader who attracts devoted followers. They consider themselves the only true Christianity, or the only true religion, and tend to separate themselves from both society at large and mainstream religious groups.

The two most horrific results of such cultic devotion in recent history were the People's Temple tragedy in Jonestown, Guyana, in 1978, and the burning of the Branch Davidian compound in Waco, Texas, in 1993. Jim Jones, paranoid and megalomaniac founder of the People's Temple, led his followers in a mass suicide in Guyana, claiming the end of the world was at hand. Over nine hundred people died. David Koresh had similar apocalyptic visions in 1993 when ATF agents raided his isolated compound near Waco, Texas, looking for illegal weapons. The fifty-one-day standoff eventually ended with a huge conflagration that killed Koresh and eighty-two of his followers, including many children.

While few cults end in such tragedy, the People's Temple and the Branch Davidians shared many of the same characteristics as other groups. Almost all are led by a leader who demands total or near-total devotion, and claims to speak for God. Most claim to be the only true religion, suffering opposition and persecution from "unbelievers." Many encourage or even insist that followers turn over their resources and cut ties with family and friends. The group itself, not your natural parents, represents your true family. Devotion to former family must cease and ultimate allegiance given to your new spiritual family.

Where could such a claim come from?

Well, apparently it came from Jesus himself. Jesus made some remarkably strong statements about family allegiance. For example, on one occasion he apparently refused to meet with his own family, claiming that his disciples were his true brothers and sisters (Mk 3:33-35//Mt 12:48-49//Lk 8:21). On another occasion he said that unless you *hate* your own family, you were not worthy to be his disciple (Lk 14:26; cf. Mt 10:37). Was Jesus behaving badly when he redefined family relationships?

DID JESUS REPUDIATE FAMILY RELATIONSHIPS?

"Honor your father and your mother"—this is number five of the Ten Commandments (Ex 20:12; Deut 5:16). Anything that makes God's Top Ten List must be pretty important. Don't forget these Ten Commandments were written in stone (literally) by God's own hand. Honoring parents ranks right up there with not worshiping other gods or committing murder. Just how important it is can be seen in the penalties prescribed in the Old Testament for *not* honoring your parents. A rebellious and disobedient son was to be stoned to death (Deut 21:18-21)—a bit worse than having your iPhone taken away or being grounded for a week. The punishment for cursing your father or mother was likewise death (Ex 21:17).

Jesus himself emphasized the importance of honoring parents. In one of his blistering attacks on the religious leaders, he pointed out that they claimed to keep the commandments of God but then found clever ways around them. For example, they used the law of *Corban*—an Aramaic word meaning "offering" or "vow"—to protect their personal property. When their aged parents needed support, they would say, "Sorry, that money is *Corban*—set apart for God— so you can't touch it." In the guise of piety and devotion, they refused to help their parents and so broke the fifth commandment. Jesus condemns their hypocrisy: "Thus you nullify the word of God by your tradition that you have handed down" (Mk 7:9-13//Mt 15:3-7).

But did Jesus practice what he preached? At times he seems to have shown disregard for his own family.

Ditching his parents. Take, for example, the only story about Jesus from his childhood (Lk 2:41-52). Jesus was twelve years old, and his parents had taken him to Jerusalem for Passover. This was an important rite of passage for a Jewish boy as he approached his thirteenth birthday, when he was viewed as an adult with reference to the Jewish law. After celebrating the Passover, the family began the four- or five-day return trip from Jerusalem to Nazareth. They were evidently traveling in a caravan of family and friends, and his parents Joseph and Mary assumed Jesus was with his buddies. A day into the journey they realized he was gone!

This must have been terrifying for his parents. Losing a child is every parent's nightmare. I remember losing our oldest son at Disneyland when he was about six years old. I thought he was with my wife, and she thought he was with me. Suddenly "the happiest place on earth" became the scariest. Fortunately, my son had the presence of mind to seek out an employee and tell him he was lost. We caught sight of him as the employee was accompanying him to the "lost parents" office.

While our son accidentally got lost, Jesus seems to have intentionally done so. When his parents found him in the temple courts in Jerusalem, he was listening to the religious sages and asking them questions. His mother put the blame squarely on Jesus: "Son, why have you treated us like this? Your father and I have been anxiously searching for you" (Lk 2:48). Jesus' response—"Didn't you know I had to be in my Father's house?"—may be a profound revelation of Jesus' Father-Son relationship with God, but from his parents' perspective it's quite a slam. Mary says, "You've disrespected *your father and me.*" Jesus responds essentially, "Sorry, I had to be with my *real* father." This doesn't seem much like honoring his father and mother. As if to temper Jesus' answer, Luke, the narrator, adds that Jesus subsequently returned to Nazareth with his parents "and was obedient to them" (Lk 2:51). Luke wants to emphasize that Jesus *was not* a disrespectful son after all.

Repudiating his family. Jesus' casual attitude toward family loyalty apparently continued into adulthood. At about age thirty he left the family carpentry business to set off as a preacher. This kind of itinerate preaching would certainly not pay the bills or support his aging mother. His four brothers were skeptical of this career, and John's Gospel tells us they did not believe in him (Jn 7:5).

Jesus' call to his disciples to leave home and family would also have been shocking and offensive to his contemporaries. In Mark 1:16-20 (//Mt 4:18-22) Jesus calls two pairs of fishermen brothers to be his disciples, Peter and Andrew, and James and John. They leave everything behind and follow him. It is said that James and John "left their father Zebedee in the boat with the hired men and followed him" (Mk 1:20; cf. Mt 4:19-22; Lk 5:11). A son's loyalty was first and foremost to his father and family. To forsake this to follow a dubious itinerate preacher would have been viewed as impudent and rebellious.

At times Jesus seemed intentionally to alienate his family. The Synoptic Gospels describe a scene when his family came to speak with him. They were justifiably worried. Jesus had been working so hard that he and his disciples barely had time to eat or sleep. His family was concerned and went to bring him home. Their conclusion: "He is out of his mind" (Mk 3:20-21). They think Jesus is crazy and are ready to have him committed. When they arrive, Jesus is inside a house meeting with his disciples. The family sends word: "Your mother and brothers are outside looking for you." Yet instead of going outside to talk with them, Jesus responds, "Who are my mother and brothers?" He points to his disciples sitting around him and says, "Here are my mother and my brothers! Whoever does God's will is my brother and sister and mother" (Mk 3:31-35//Mt 12:46-50//Lk 8:19-21). In a culture where respect for family, and especially parents, was immeasurably high, this would have sounded like a repudiation.

In a similar vein, Jesus told his disciples not to call anyone on earth "father," since they had only one Father, and he is in heaven (Mt 23:9). When a man who desired to follow Jesus wanted to first go and bury his father (who had presumably just died), Jesus said, "Let the dead bury their own dead" (Mt 8:21-22//Lk 9:59-60). The highest calling for a son would be to give his father a noble burial, yet Jesus apparently dismisses this as irrelevant. When another would-be disciple asks if he can go and say goodbye to his family, Jesus responds, "No one who puts a hand to the plow and looks back is fit for service in the kingdom of God" (Lk 9:62). This would have seemed shockingly disrespectful in first-century Judaism.

Demanding hate for one's family? But it gets even worse. In his most astonishing statement about the cost of discipleship Jesus said that those who wanted to be his disciple would have to *hate* their father and mother, wife and children, and brothers and sisters (Lk 14:26). This seems pretty radical, even cultlike. The saying is so shocking Matthew apparently softened it: "Anyone who loves their father or mother *more than me* is not worthy of me" (Mt 10:37).

The blessings of leaving family. Jesus also spoke indirectly about repudiating family. After the episode of the rich young ruler, where this man found it impossible to sell everything he had and follow Jesus, Peter spoke for the other disciples when he said, "We have left all we had to follow you!" Jesus responds, "Truly I tell you, . . . no one who has left home or wife or brothers or sisters or parents or children for the sake of the kingdom of God will fail to receive many times as much in this age, and in the age to come eternal life" (Lk 18:29-30//Mk 10:29-30//Mt 19:29). Leaving family for the sake of Jesus is a virtue that will be rewarded both in this life and the life to come.

Repudiating marriage? One of Jesus' most perplexing comments comes after his teaching about divorce in Matthew 19. After teaching that remarriage after divorce results in adultery (Mt 19:9), his disciples are astonished and ask, "If this is the situation between a husband and wife, it is better not to marry" (Mt 19:10). Jesus responds:

> Not all men *can accept* this statement, but *only* those to whom it has been given. For there are eunuchs who were born that way from their mother's womb; and there are eunuchs who were made eunuchs by men; and there are *also* eunuchs

who made themselves eunuchs for the sake of the kingdom of heaven. He who is able to accept *this*, let him accept *it*. (Mt 19:11-12 NASB)

Making yourself a eunuch apparently means castration. "Struggling with sexual temptation?" Jesus says, "If you are willing, cut it off!" At least one early church leader, the third-century theologian Origen, is said to have done this in quite literal obedience to this passage.[3] Many commentators, however, suggest that the passage more likely means to live a life of voluntary celibacy.[4] The NIV reads, "There are those who choose to live like eunuchs for the sake of the kingdom of heaven."

In either case, one wonders why Jesus would encourage celibacy for the kingdom of God. Can't someone serve God just as effectively as a married person?

So was Jesus antifamily? Should his followers cut themselves off from their own family to follow him? Should they remain celibate and avoid marriage? In light of Jesus' statements recorded here, it seems odd that groups espousing Christian values—Focus on the Family and Family Research Council—have such a strong emphasis on family ties. Would Jesus have instead affirmed the Family Repudiation Council?

Resolving the Paradox: True Family in the Kingdom of God

Jesus' affirmation of the family. So was Jesus opposed to the traditional family unit? Did he dismiss the importance of family loyalty? Did he repudiate marriage? There is certainly evidence to the contrary. Jesus extolled faithfulness to the marriage covenant and spoke against divorce, which broke this covenant relationship. As we have seen, he condemned the religious leaders for finding ways around caring for their aging parents. He exalted the status of children and encouraged his followers to welcome them.

Yet we must not soft-pedal Jesus' statements about where true loyalties lie. As we have done throughout this book, we need to understand Jesus' teaching about family in the context of his central message: the coming of the kingdom of God.

True family loyalty in God's kingdom. By proclaiming the arrival of God's kingdom through his own words and actions, Jesus was declaring war. It was a spiritual war against Satan, sin, death and all the results of evil in the world. His exorcisms, healings and conflicts with the religious leaders were all skirmishes in this war. It is impossible to stay neutral in war. As Jesus himself said, "Whoever is not with me is against me" (Mt 12:30//Lk 11:23). There is no neutral ground.

And wars often turn brother against brother. The American Civil War saw fathers, sons, brothers, uncles and cousins facing each other on the field of battle. Wars demand a decision related to allegiance. Was it family first or nation first? When the command came to attack, family allegiances often dissolved and brother raised weapon against brother.

Jesus said he came to bring fire to the earth—the purging presence of the Spirit of God. This fire would purify and refine the righteous, but it would burn up and destroy the wicked. When Jesus commissioned his twelve disciples and sent them out to preach, he warned them of the danger of family betrayal: "I am sending you out like sheep among wolves. . . . Brother will betray brother to death, and a father his child; children will rebel against their parents and have them put to death. You will be hated by everyone because of me" (Mt 10:16, 21-22; cf. Mk 13:12; Lk 21:16).

Being hated by family and friends may seem harsh and extreme, but it has been the experience of many Christians whose newfound faith has put them at odds with their own culture and with those they love. While this kind of family hatred may be rare in the West, it is more common around the world.

Consider the story of Mohammed, a Nigerian Muslim from the Fulani people, who was excelling at a young age in his study of the Qur'an.[5] Since he was a star pupil, his father sent him away to several elite schools for advanced studies in Islam. At the age of twenty-two, as Mohammed was making plans to go to Saudi Arabia for further studies, he began having disturbing dreams about demons. His father took him to the local witch doctor, who concluded he was under the spell of witches and gave him potions to ward off evil spirits. The dreams persisted, however, until finally a man came to him in his dreams. The man identified himself as Isa (Jesus), rescued him from the demons and told Mohammed to place his faith in him. In time Mohammed found a Christian in a nearby village. The man brought him to a pastor, who shared the gospel with him and led him to faith in Jesus.

When his father found out that his son had become an infidel, he was furious. He warned Mohammed to give up this heresy or be disowned. Mohammed refused and was made a pariah in the village. His father brought him before the village elders and forced him to drink poison. When Mohammed survived the poison, his father banished him from the village, ordering relatives to follow and kill him. His relatives shot him with a poison-tipped arrow. On the brink of death, Mohammed was discovered by a hunter from another village and taken to a hospital, where he was able to recover from his wounds. Jesus' prediction that "brother will betray brother to death, and a father his child" (Mk 13:12) certainly came true in Mohammed's life.

Many similar stories have been told of those turning to Christ from Muslim, Buddhist, Hindu or animistic faiths. Though some families are accepting, many others reject, ostracize, disown and even threaten violence against those who would turn away from the family faith. (The same sentiments, of course, can go the other way, with Christian families rejecting those who turn to other faiths.) In situations like this the social pressure to reject your newfound faith and return to the security of the old is enormous. Why cut yourself off from family, friends, business prospects, marriage opportunities and any hope for success in life? In many places ethnic identity is integrally linked to religion. To be a member of the Fulani tribe is to be a Muslim. To be a high-caste Indian is to be a Hindu. In contexts like this, to give up your religious tradition is to die to your personal identity, to be cut off from everything that you have and are. This is not an easy decision to make.

We have good friends who lived for a number of years in Germany working as missionaries among Muslim guest workers. They were working especially with Kurds, a minority ethnic group that has often been persecuted by other Muslims and so was somewhat more open to the gospel than other Muslims. After several years of ministry, some responded to the gospel and became believers in Jesus. They expressed a desire to be baptized. Our friends wrote an excited newsletter, expressing their joy at this turn of events. They were welcoming new family members! We waited expectantly to hear how things went.

Yet with the next newsletter came somber news. At the last minute the new believers had backed out. To publicly announce their Christian baptism was just too much too soon. They could not bring themselves to do what seemed to be a repudiation of their family and cultural identity.

Most of these new believers were eventually baptized and did publicly proclaim their faith. But the story illustrates well the extreme cost of discipleship. In many contexts around the world one's religion is inseparably connected to culture and family. To follow Jesus can result in rejection by spouses, parents and children, and can feel like a denial of everything you are. Where do you turn when you lose your family? The answer, Jesus says, is you turn to your real family, the family of God.

It was the same in the Greco-Roman world of the New Testament. The world of the first century was strongly group oriented (as opposed to individual oriented). People found their identity in their relationship to others, rather than through individual accomplishment. And in this context the family or clan, with the father as the patriarchal head, was the primary focus of self-identity and of allegiance. In his book *When the Church Was a Family*, Joseph Hellerman emphasizes this point with reference to the church:

> Family served as the primary locus of relational loyalty for persons in the strong-group social matrix of the New Testament world. Those who followed Jesus were to exercise primary allegiance to a new family—just as Jesus himself had done: "Whoever does the will of God is my brother and sister and mother" (Mark 3:35).[6]

Social and family life was also closely linked to religious traditions. If you were invited to a birthday party, it would be held in a pagan temple. If your boss decided to give you a promotion and throw you a party, the celebration might be held in the temple of your trade guild. Pagan temples were the Chuck E. Cheeses and the Dave & Buster's of the ancient world. If you wished to marry into a prominent family, you would be expected to worship their pagan gods. If you bought a nice steak in the marketplace, it likely would have been offered already as a sacrifice to a pagan god. (Since the gods didn't eat much, the temple priests made a healthy profit selling the meat in the marketplace.)

In the letters to seven churches in the book of Revelation, the church at Thyatira is warned against a woman named Jezebel, who is encouraging Christians to join in immoral pagan ceremonies and to eat food sacrificed to idols (Rev 2:20-22). "Jezebel" is probably a nickname for this woman, comparing her to the wicked queen who killed God's prophets and led Israel into idol worship (see 1 Kings

16:31; 18:13). John warns, "Don't follow her!" Such compromise is pagan worship and will result in God's judgment.

Emperor worship was also becoming an important part of civic life in the Roman empire of the first and second centuries. All citizens loyal to the government would be expected to participate in the worship of *dea Roma*—the deified personification of the Roman state—as well as worship of the Roman emperor. Imagine if, instead of saying the Pledge of Allegiance every morning, kids in America were required to say a prayer of worship to the president. Not to do so would get you expelled. In such a context, why not listen to the voices of moderation and compromise? Why not worship *both* Caesar and Jesus?

But for believers there was only one true Lord. To worship Caesar meant to repudiate Jesus as Lord. With this radical dichotomy in mind, Jesus affirmed that loyalty to God and his kingdom superseded all human loyalties and commitments. Our first allegiance is not to those with whom we share family, ethnic or national identity. It is to our creator God and his purposes in the world. Our *true family* is all who share this covenant relationship. Jesus models this by pointing to his disciples, rather than his mother and siblings, as his true mother, brothers and sisters, "Whoever does the will of my Father in heaven is my brother and sister and mother" (Mt 12:50; Mk 3:35; Lk 8:21).

Throughout the New Testament, believers are called "brothers and sisters" (Greek: *adelphoi*). This is no trite address ("Hey, bro!"). It means that our *real* family is those who are part of the family of God, his spiritual children. To be "born again" (Jn 3:3-7) means to be adopted as a child of God (Rom 8:15; Gal 3:26; 1 Jn 3:1-2, 10), creating an allegiance to a new family that supersedes all other allegiances.

This kingdom-family mindset provides the context for other sayings of Jesus. When Jesus shockingly refuses to grant permission for a potential disciple to give his father a noble burial (Lk 9:59-60//

Mt 8:21-22) or even to say goodbye to parents (Lk 9:61-62), he is emphasizing the necessity of radical commitment to the kingdom. "The dead" who will bury the dead probably means the spiritually dead, those who have rejected the message of the kingdom of God. Jesus here echoes the Elijah/Elisha narrative, where Elijah *permits* Elisha to return and say goodbye to his parents before setting off as Elijah's disciple (1 Kings 19:19-21). The point is that Jesus' call to discipleship is far more urgent and important than even the prophetic ministry of Elijah. This is because the salvation that was *predicted* by the prophets is coming to *fulfillment* through Jesus' words and actions.

The rhetorical power of hyperbole. What about Jesus' apparent command to "hate" parents, spouses and siblings? How can we square this with Jesus' command to love even our enemies? If believers are *commanded* to love their enemies, how can they show any less love for their physical relatives?

Though this remains a difficult passage, the best answer is that Jesus is using his characteristic hyperbole to bring home the seriousness of the situation. As when he speaks about giant planks of wood protruding from one's eye (an impossibility) and camels going through a needle's eye (equally absurd), Jesus shocks to get his hearer's attention.

Hate can certainly mean "love less." This is the case, for example, in Deuteronomy 21:15, where a situation is described in which a man has two wives, one whom he loves and the other he "hates" (KJV). The text means that he loves one wife more than the other. Similarly, in Genesis 29:31 we learn that Leah was "hated" (ESV; NIV has "not loved") by Jacob. The Hebrew word translated "hated" can mean "loved less," as the previous verse confirms: "His love for Rachel was greater than his love for Leah" (Gen 29:30).

Jesus' point is not that we should actually hate our parents, spouses or siblings. It is that such human relationships are of little significance when compared to true spiritual relationships in the kingdom of God. Matthew's version of the saying, which speaks of loving family "more than me" (Mt 10:37), may be closer to what Jesus actually meant. But it is far less powerful in its rhetorical force than the saying in Luke, which speaks of "hating" family. Hyperbole is meant to get our attention. I might say to my kids, "If you don't get home before midnight, *you will be grounded for life*." This, of course, is absurd (who would want kids in the house for the rest of your life!). My hyperbole, though not to be taken literally, communicates how serious I am. Jesus wants to point out how deadly serious this is.

The use of hyperbole also explains Jesus' command not to call anyone on earth "father" (Mt 23:9). Jesus can hardly mean that children should address their fathers by their first names or call them "brother" instead. The question is rather one of allegiance. As the patriarchal head of the family, the father received absolute loyalty and full submission from the family. In the same way, family loyalty now belongs to God alone, the patriarchal head of the family of believers—"for you have one Father, and he is in heaven" (Mt 23:9). The parallel statement confirms this meaning: "Nor are you to be called instructors, for you have one Instructor, the Messiah" (Mt 23:10). This cannot mean that there should be no teachers in the church, since teachers are affirmed throughout the New Testament. It means, rather, that we have only one authoritative teacher, and that is Jesus. All others are subordinate to him.

To place the things of this world—whether worldly possessions or human relationships—above loyalty to the kingdom of God has enormous, even eternal, consequences. *Hate* is not too strong a word in such circumstances. As F. F. Bruce says, "If 'hating' one's relatives is felt to be a shocking idea, it was meant to be shocking, to shock the hearers into a sense of the imperious demands of the kingdom of God."[7]

CONCLUSION

Years ago, during my doctoral studies in Scotland, I traveled to Romania to teach a course on the Gospels to a group of Romanian students and pastors. Apart from outreach trips to Mexico in my youth, it was my first extended time working with Christians from another culture. It was December 1990, a year after the Romanian revolution that overthrew the ruthless dictator Nicolae Ceauşescu, and the country was still suffering from severe economic hardships from his rule. I had a life-changing trip. My students were like sponges, eager to learn as much as they could about Jesus and the Gospels. I taught in various cities, preached in numerous churches and spent long hours into the night over coffee discussing the Bible, theology and politics with my new friends. I was amazed at the welcome I received. Though the families I stayed with had almost no money, they welcomed me like family. Wherever I went, I was treated like royalty. They had obviously purchased the best food they could afford, and each meal brought it out for me. I remember waking up in one home and walking into the kitchen. I saw the family eating a meager breakfast of toast and tea. Immediately upon seeing me, the table was cleared and new food was put out for me. I tried to say, no, the toast was fine, but they would not have it. I was an honored guest.

As I was preparing to fly home, the Romanian airline Tarom went on strike on the one-year anniversary of the revolution (I never quite figured out why you go on strike to celebrate a revolution!). After a grueling overnight train from Timişoara to the capital Bucharest, I arrived to find an empty airport and no flights leaving. I wouldn't be able to get out for days. International phone connections were terrible, and I couldn't even reach my wife in Scotland to tell her what was happening. I went to the US Embassy, but they said, "Sorry," they didn't help travelers. My money was almost gone.

Finally, I called a Christian brother named Cristi, who I had met briefly when I arrived in the country. He dropped everything, picked me up and took me to his home, and he and his wife fed me dinner. He worked out a plan. I would take the overnight train across the country five hundred miles from Bucharest to Budapest, Hungary, and would then fly home from Hungary. Cristi took me to the train station, purchased my ticket (with money he could not afford) and gave me detailed instructions on how to navigate the train system. He stood with me on the platform for a long time in the frigid December weather waiting for the train. We talked about our families, our ministries and our future hopes for Romania. When the train finally arrived, he helped me carry my bags on board, tried to stuff more money in my hand (which I refused) and gave me a traditional Romanian kiss on both cheeks. "Godspeed," he said. I should not have been surprised. After all, he was my brother.

Since that time I've been on various trips abroad and frequently experienced this kind of family love and hospitality. This is just what Jesus predicted. Remember Jesus' statement in Mark 10:29-30. He has just explained the enormous cost of discipleship by telling the rich young ruler to sell all he has and to follow him. When Peter responds, "We have left everything to follow you," Jesus speaks of the rewards for such sacrifice:

> "Truly I tell you," Jesus replied, "no one who has left home or brothers or sisters or mother or father or children or fields for me and the gospel will fail to receive a hundred times as much in this present age: homes, brothers, sisters, mothers, children and fields—along with persecutions—and in the age to come eternal life." (Mk 10:29-30)

Notice the most surprising part of this promise. For those who have experienced persecution and lost everything in this world, including families and homes, Jesus promises not only eternal life in the future but many more brothers, sisters, mothers, children, homes and fields *in this present age!* How can this be? The answer is that to receive the kingdom of God means adoption into the largest family in the world, with all of its vast resources. The generosity and hospitality I experienced in Romania and elsewhere is just a fringe benefit of being part of the family of God. With that in mind let's never forget the struggles, needs and suffering of our *true* brothers and sisters around the world.

RACIST OR INCLUSIVIST?

GENTILE DOGS AND
OTHER RIFFRAFF

IN A CLASSIC EPISODE OF the television show *The Office*, Michael Scott, regional manager of the Dunder Mifflin Paper Company, becomes frustrated when a consultant comes in to conduct a day of diversity training. The episode, called "Diversity Day," is painful to watch, as Michael shows blissful ignorance of his own racism. He assumes that the consultant's name, "Mr. Brown," must be a ruse to trap them into making racist remarks, since no African American would have that name. He asks Oscar, a Mexican American, if there is a less offensive term than "Mexican" he would like to be called, since that term has "certain connotations." When a coworker from India has to excuse herself to meet a client, he expresses frustration since "if you leave, we'll only have two left"—meaning one African American and one Hispanic (the rest of the workers are white). Though Michael insists the training is unnecessary because his office "is very advanced in racial awareness," the consultant informs him that the training is a result of complaints about Michael's own racially charged Chris Rock impersonation. Comedy is usually funniest when it hits dangerously close to home, and this episode is no exception. Most of us have heard the kind of subtle and not-so-subtle racist sentiments that Michael expresses.

RACISM IN JESUS' DAY

Racism, or at least ethnocentricity, was alive and well in the ancient world. Though such prejudice was not generally based on physical features like skin color, people looked down on others of different ethnicities and ancestry. Racism is often provoked by xenophobia (no, not fear of the warrior princess Xena)—fear of that which is foreign (*xenos*) or different or strange. Most ancient peoples viewed themselves as superior—the "true" people—in contrast to outsiders who were inferior. The Greeks coined the term *barbarians*, an onomatopoetic term for those less-civilized nations whose strange languages sounded like babbling: "bar, bar, bar." Mary Beard, professor of classics at Cambridge, writes, "The Greeks painted a contemptuous picture of the Persians as trousered, decadent softies who wore far too much perfume. Then the Romans came along and, minus the trousers, said much the same about the Greeks."[1]

Jews too considered themselves superior to others. They were, after all, the chosen people of God. Hatred for others was not uncommon. The apocryphal book of Sirach (2nd c. B.C.) describes this loathing. The high priest Simon pronounces a blessing over the nation Israel and a curse upon surrounding enemies:

> Two nations my soul detests,
>   and the third is not even a people:
> Those who live in Seir, and the Philistines,
>   and the foolish people that live in Shechem. (Sirach
>   50:25-26 NRSV)

The people of Seir are the Edomites to the south of Israel, the descendants of Esau, Jacob's brother. The Philistines are the sea peoples to the west, and the "foolish people" of Shechem are the Samaritans. Jews especially hated Samaritans, since they viewed them not only as half-breeds but also as practicing a corrupt and heretical form of Judaism. According to this statement, the Samaritans can't really be detested since they are "not even a people." I am reminded of how some people have referred to the Palestinians as "not really a people," since they have never had a nation of their own. If they don't exist, how can they have any rights?

WAS JESUS RACIST?

Did Jesus share the ethnocentricity of his people? There is certainly evidence that Jesus favored his own Jewish people over others. He called the Gentiles "dogs" and told a Gentile woman, "I was sent only to the lost sheep of Israel" (Mt 15:24). He told his disciples only to share the good news of salvation with the Jewish people and not to go to the Gentiles. Only after the Jewish leadership rejected his message (and had him crucified!) did Jesus tell his followers to expand their outreach to non-Jews. Could Jesus' actions be called "racist"?

Gentile dogs and other riffraff. One of the most surprising statements of Jesus in the Gospels occurs when a Gentile woman approaches him and asks him to heal her demon-possessed daughter (Mt 15:21-28//Mk 7:24-30). Jesus has ventured into Gentile territory, the region of Tyre and Sidon, in Phoenicia north of Israel along the Mediterranean coast. Why Jesus went there is not clear. It may have been to get away from the region of Galilee because of threats against him by Herod Antipas, the Jewish king over Galilee. Herod had executed John the Baptist and was increasingly worried about Jesus. Or perhaps Jesus wanted to get away from the religious leaders, who were increasingly harassing him. In any event, he wants to be alone with his disciples to continue their training. Mark says, "He entered a house and did not want anyone to know it" (Mk 7:24).

But Jesus' reputation as a healer precedes him, and a woman from the region hears about his arrival and comes to ask him for help. She repeatedly begs Jesus to heal her daughter, who is demon possessed. According to Matthew, Jesus first simply ignores her request. When she persists, the annoyed disciples get frustrated and ask Jesus to send her away. In response, Jesus tells her he is only here for his own people: "I was sent only to the lost sheep of Israel" (Mt 15:24). This sounds rather callous. Where is the inclusive nature of God's salvation?

But when she continues to beg, it gets even worse. Jesus shockingly says, "It is not right to take the children's bread and toss it to the dogs" (Mt 15:26). The "children" here are the people of Israel, who are often referred to in the Hebrew Scriptures as God's children. "Dogs" was a derogatory way Jews referred to Gentiles. The Jews did not view dogs as loyal and loving pets, but as filthy scavengers. The reader is stunned to hear Jesus refer to Gentiles as wild beasts rather than as people. It may be true that Jesus softens his words a bit by using a diminutive form of the word dog (*kynarion*) instead of the more common one (*kyōn*). This could be his way of adapting to the Gentile context, where dogs *were* kept as pets. In either case, however, it still sounds like an insult. Jesus, like the famous "Soup Nazi" on *Seinfeld*, says, "No soup [bread] for you!"

The woman, however, will not be put off. She agrees with Jesus' point that the bread was baked for the children, but then she responds: "Even the dogs eat the crumbs that fall from their master's table." She accepts the derogatory epithet "dog" but then asks for the rights of dogs—to be fed! Jesus is impressed by this persistence and grants the healing: "Woman, you have great faith! Your request is granted." The daughter, we learn, was instantly healed (Mt 15:28).

This episode is unique in several ways. For one thing, this is the only time in the Gospels that Jesus loses a debate. He concedes that the woman is right and changes his mind. The surprising irony is that Jesus always *wins* in debates against the powerful, male religious leaders. But here he "loses" against a woman, and a Gentile woman at that!

There are two main interpretations of what happens here. Some commentators claim that Jesus had no desire or intention to help the woman, but that her clever answer changed his mind. Jesus examines his own ethnocentricity and then modifies it. This is possible, but a better way to read it is that Jesus is intentionally provoking her faith. This fits the tone of the Gospels, where Jesus is always in charge, guiding events and conversations in the direction he wants them to go.

Jesus wants to see the woman claim what is rightfully hers, which is access to God's salvation. But he does so provocatively. With the disciples looking on, he answers her request with a common Jewish stereotype: The Gentiles are despicable "dogs" who are outside of God's family and the scope of salvation. When Jesus said this, the disciples no doubt nodded in agreement and uttered a hearty amen. The woman's response, though a humble one, brings the Gentiles into the household as those who receive the same bread as the children. Jesus responds, "Good answer!" Jesus is impressed because this Gentile woman shows greater awareness of God's plan for all humanity than the religious leaders of Israel.

It is important to note that in the woman's analogy there is still an order to salvation. The gospel goes first to the Jews and then to the Gentiles. As Jesus says in Mark's version of this episode, "*First* let the children eat . . ." (Mk 7:27). We will discuss this priority of salvation more below.

Selective evangelism. There are other indications of Jesus' preference for the Jews. For one thing, he chose an inner circle of twelve (Jewish) disciples. As we have seen before, the number twelve likely symbolizes the twelve tribes of Israel and so represents a renewal of the nation Israel.

In Matthew's Gospel, when Jesus sends the Twelve out on their mission, he explicitly tells them *not* to go to the Gentiles or the Samaritans: "Do not go among the Gentiles or enter any town of the Samaritans. Go rather to the lost sheep of Israel" (Mt 10:5-6; cf. Mt 15:24). In his conversation with the Samaritan woman at the well in John, he tells her, "You Samaritans worship what you do not know; we worship what we do know, for salvation is from the Jews" (Jn 4:22). How do we explain this selective offer of salvation? To answer this question, we have to answer the question of Israel's role in God's plan of salvation.

TO THE JEW FIRST

Genesis 12 marks a key turning point in the biblical story, as God calls Abraham from his home and family to go to a place God will show him. God promises to bless Abraham, to give him a land, to make from him a great nation and to bless all nations through him (Gen 12:1-3). Through Abraham, God will create a nation—Israel— and through that nation he would bless all nations. The Old Testament repeatedly refers to this special relationship with Israel. Deuteronomy 14:2 reads, "For you are a people holy to the LORD your God. Out of all the peoples on the face of the earth, the LORD has chosen you to be his treasured possession."

As God's chosen people, Israel had a special mission. The nation was intended to be a light to the rest of the nations, a place where the people of the world could come to see and experience the glory of the one true God. In Isaiah 40–55 we see this role repeatedly emphasized:

He said to me, "You are my servant,
  Israel, in whom I will display my splendor." . . .
"I will also make you a light for the Gentiles,
  that my salvation may reach to the ends of the earth."
    (Is 49:3, 6)

When Jesus began his ministry, his first role was to call Israel to respond, to be the light that God intended the nation to be. This is why Jesus chose twelve apostles, representing the twelve tribes of Israel. This is why he sent them at first only to the lost sheep of Israel (Mt 10:6; 15:24). Only after salvation had been achieved through his life, death and resurrection does Jesus give the Twelve his Great Commission to make disciples of *all nations* (Mt 28:18-20). Israel's role was to be salt and light, God's ambassadors to take this message to the ends of the earth (Acts 1:8).

This vision and mission is seen clearly in the ministry of the apostle Paul. Whatever town he entered, he would go to the synagogue and proclaim the message of salvation *first to the Jews*. In this way he was calling Israel to respond and be the light they were intended to be. Generally, a small number of Jews would respond to the message. When others rejected it, Paul would turn to the Gentiles. Paul's ministry in Pisidian Antioch is characteristic. After an initially successful ministry, the majority of the Jews there reject the message:

> Then Paul and Barnabas answered them boldly: "We had to speak the word of God to you first. Since you reject it and do not consider yourselves worthy of eternal life, we now turn to the Gentiles. For this is what the Lord has commanded us:
>
> "'I have made you a light for the Gentiles,
>   that you may bring salvation to the ends of the earth.'"
>   (Acts 13:46-47; citing Is 49:6)

After Paul calls out the righteous remnant from Israel, he turns and offers salvation to the Gentiles. Though Paul says things like, "We now turn to the Gentiles" (Acts 13:46) or "From now on I will go to the Gentiles" (Acts 18:6), he only means that from now on *in this place*. Everywhere he goes after this, he preaches first to the Jews and then to the Gentiles. This is because the Jews have priority in God's salvation. They are to be salt and light—a transforming presence—for the rest of the world. As Paul says in Romans 1:16: "I am not ashamed of the gospel, because it is the power of God that brings salvation to everyone who believes: *first to the Jew, then to the Gentile*" (italics added).

RADICAL INCLUSION

Though Jesus occasionally spoke of Israel's priority with reference to God's salvation, he expressed even more forcefully God's intention to bring salvation to all people everywhere. Though many in Israel saw salvation as their own unique inheritance, Jesus affirmed that the message of salvation that came through Israel was good news for the whole world.

We have already seen Jesus' commendation of a Syrophoenician woman for her persistent faith. A similar scene occurs when a Roman centurion asks Jesus to heal his servant (Mt 8:5-13//Lk 7:1-10).[2] When Jesus expresses his willingness to come, the man—cognizant that pious Jews did not enter the homes of (impure) Gentiles—affirms that Jesus has the ability to simply say the word and heal the man from a distance. Jesus is astonished and announces, "I have not found anyone in Israel with such great faith" (Mt 8:10//Lk 7:9). In Matthew's version of the event, Jesus adds an indictment against the religious leaders:

> I say to you that many will come from the east and the west, and will take their places at the feast with Abraham, Isaac and Jacob in the kingdom of heaven. But the subjects of the kingdom will be thrown outside, into the darkness, where there will be weeping and gnashing of teeth. (Mt 8:11-12; cf. Lk 13:28-29)

Jesus here predicts an astonishing reversal. The insiders—the religious elite of Israel—will find themselves on the outside, while the outsiders—Gentiles—will feast at the messianic banquet with the patriarchs in the kingdom of God. This is a message of radical inclusion that would have been astonishing to Jesus' contemporaries.

There are many other passages that illustrate Jesus' message of inclusion. This is the central theme of Jesus' inaugural sermon in his hometown of Nazareth.

The Nazareth sermon (Lk 4:14-30). "Hometown Boy Makes Good!" could have been the headline of the *Nazareth Gazette* on the Sabbath when Jesus returned to his hometown. He had been moving throughout the villages of the Galilee and had gained quite a reputation as a dynamic teacher, healer and exorcist. Now he was given the opportunity to give the sermon in the synagogue Sabbath service—quite an honor for a young man.

There is an air of excitement and a hushed awe as Jesus enters the synagogue, his disciples trailing behind. A young boy whispers excitedly to his father, "There he is!" and the father places his arm on the boy's shoulder to quiet him. The disciples disperse to find seats in the crowded room while Jesus moves to the front. The synagogue attendant, an older distinguished man with a gray beard, hands him a beautiful parchment scroll of Isaiah, the pride of the Nazareth synagogue. There is the hint of a smile on the old man's face and a twinkle in his eye. He taught this boy Torah in synagogue school.

Jesus unrolls the scroll and deliberately turns to Isaiah 61. We don't know whether this passage was the prescribed liturgical reading for the day or whether Jesus selected it himself. Either way would have been remarkable. If he chose it himself, he is deliberately announcing himself to be the Messiah. If this is the prescribed reading, then God had ordained that he would read the messianic passage in the synagogue on this very day. Luke records Jesus' words:

The Spirit of the Lord is on me,
  because he has anointed me
  to proclaim good news to the poor.
He has sent me to proclaim freedom for the prisoners
  and recovery of sight for the blind,
to set the oppressed free,
  to proclaim the year of the Lord's favor. (Lk 4:18-19)

The expression "year of the Lord's favor" comes from Old Testament language related to the Year of Jubilee (Lev 25). Every fiftieth year in Israel was to be a Jubilee year, when land would be returned to its original tribal inheritance and slaves would be set free. The principle behind Jubilee was that all the land and the people belonged to God, since he had delivered Israel from slavery in Egypt. Because everything was God's, there was to be no (permanent) transfer of ownership, either of people or property. The Jubilee also established social justice, preventing the rich from gradually gobbling up all the land and enslaving the people with crushing debt.

In Isaiah 61, the prophet Isaiah took this image of Jubilee liberation and used it as a metaphor for God's final (eschatological) salvation. He predicted that one day a herald anointed by God's Spirit would proclaim a final Jubilee, which would mean good news for the poor, freedom for prisoners, liberation for the oppressed and sight for the blind.

Jesus reads this great passage on God's end-time salvation, just as generations of Jewish teachers had done in the past. But then he makes a startling announcement. Luke heightens the drama by slowing the story down and creating a narrative pause: "Then he rolled up the scroll, gave it back to the attendant and sat down. The eyes of everyone in the synagogue were fastened on him" (Lk 4:20). The rabbis would read Scripture standing up out of reverence for the text and would then sit down to teach. Jesus meticulously rolls the scroll up, hands it to the attendant and solemnly sits down. Every eye is on him. You can hear a pin drop. Jesus slowly exhales and begins to speak in slow and deliberate words: "Today this scripture is fulfilled in your hearing" (Lk 4:21).

A startled stir sweeps through the synagogue. *What?* The great prophecy of end-time liberation is coming to fulfillment now? Is Jesus claiming to be the herald of God's final salvation—the Messiah? The initial response is very positive: "All spoke well of him and were amazed at the gracious words that came from his lips. 'Isn't this Joseph's son?' they asked" (Lk 4:22). This can't be the carpenter's son, the snotty-nosed kid who grew up here with our children in Nazareth! Hometown boy makes good!

It is important to ask how the townspeople of Nazareth would have understood Isaiah's prophecy. Who were the poor? Who were the oppressed? Who were the prisoners? Their answer, of course, would be "We are!" They were suffering under the iron fist of the Roman Empire. Any movement toward independence brought swift retribution from the Roman legions. But now Jesus was announcing the great day of liberation. As the priest Zechariah had expressed a few chapters earlier in Luke's Gospel, the coming of the Messiah would mean "salvation from our enemies and from the hand of all who hate us" (Lk 1:71). This was indeed good news for the poor and oppressed!

But Jesus is about to turn the tables on his audience (figuratively; he will literally turn the tables later in Jerusalem!). The problem is not the message of liberation, which they love; it is the illustrations used to back it up. Sometimes it's said that we forget the content of a sermon and remember only the illustrations. Well, the townspeople of Nazareth never forgot (or forgave) these stories. Jesus illustrated the passage not with reference to the humble and oppressed people of Israel, but with non-Jews—Gentiles! He points out that in the days of Elijah there were many widows in Israel with great needs, but God sent the prophet to the widow of Zarephath in Sidon. And there were many people with leprosy in Israel, but God chose through the prophet Elisha to heal only the Syrian general Naaman, a Gentile (Lk 4:24-27). Jesus' point is that God's love and salvation were never intended to be Israel's exclusive right. They were for all people everywhere, and examples from the Hebrew Scriptures confirm this.

The favor and approval expressed moments earlier by the people of Nazareth suddenly evaporates, and they are filled with rage. This is heresy! They grab Jesus and drag him out of the town, attempting to push him off a cliff. He escapes, however, and walks through the crowd, going on his way (Lk 4:28-30).

The Nazareth sermon and its aftermath play out in miniature what will happen throughout the whole Gospel of Luke and its sequel, the book of Acts. Luke intentionally brings this important passage forward from a later position in Mark's Gospel (Mk 6:1-6) to highlight it at the beginning of Jesus' Galilean ministry. The point: *God's salvation is not for Israel alone. It is for all people and nations on earth.*

This theme, so well illustrated in Jesus' Nazareth sermon, appears many times in Jesus' teaching, especially in Luke's Gospel.

The parable of the good Samaritan (Lk 10:25-37). One of the most beloved of Jesus' parables is the good Samaritan. But our ears can't really hear how strange that phrase would sound to a first-century Jew. It would sound like an oxymoron: "good" and "Samaritan" just don't go together. "Lying scum Samaritan," "filthy half-breed Samaritan," "heretical, deceiving Samaritan"—these are the phrases one would expect.

So who were the Samaritans? The Samaritans considered themselves to be direct descendants of the northern Israelite tribes of Ephraim and Manasseh. According to their history, they had preserved the true worship of Yahweh, the God of Israel, through worship at their temple on Mount Gerizim. The Jews, however, considered the Samaritans to be a half-breed race that arose from intermarriage between Israelites and pagan colonists brought in after the Assyrian conquest of the northern kingdom of Israel. Their religion was a false and heretical version of Judaism, what we might call a "cult," and their temple a place of false worship. Hatred between Jews and Samaritans reached a climax in 128 B.C., when the Jewish king John Hyrcanus marched north and destroyed Shechem and the Samaritan temple on Mount Gerizim, forcing many Samaritans to convert to Judaism.

In Jesus' day, Jews loathed Samaritans, and the feelings were mutual. Stories abounded of atrocities on both sides of the border. So when Jesus insisted on traveling through Samaritan territory and then his disciples found him talking to a Samaritan woman, they were naturally surprised (Jn 4). It was viewed as impious for a Jewish rabbi to be seen talking to a woman at all, let alone a despised Samaritan woman.

Equally shocking was when Jesus used a parable about a Samaritan to illustrate what it meant to be a true neighbor. The context was a question from a Jewish expert in the law, who asked Jesus, "Teacher, what must I do to inherit eternal life?" (Lk 10:25). The man asks one of the most profound questions of life. What is the key to life with God forever? When Jesus asks what the law teaches, the man replies with the two greatest commandments: love God and love others (Deut 6:5; Lev 19:18). Jesus commends him for the correct answer, yet the man wants clarification. So he asks, "And who is my neighbor?" Although he asks, "Who is my neighbor?" he really means "Who is *not* my neighbor?" (Lk 10:29). He's looking for loopholes. Who do I need to love and who don't I need to love in order to inherit eternal life?

Jesus responds with the parable. It begins on the stark desert road from Jerusalem to Jericho, a treacherous path that drops twenty-five hundred feet in seventeen miles. This desolate road was a dangerous place, the haunt of robbers and bandits. In the parable a Jewish man traveling the road is mugged, beat up and left for dead. In turn, two men pass by on the road. They are both clergy members, one a Levite and the other a priest. But instead of helping the man, they pass by on the other side. They, no doubt, had good reasons for not stopping. This might be a trap, with bandits lurking nearby. I tell my teenage kids never to stop for strangers while driving alone! You just never know. But these are meant to be Israel's religious leaders, who should be the first to show compassion.

While we are certainly meant to be surprised that two religious leaders would not stop to help, Jesus' original hearers may not have been *too* surprised. After all, priests could be a bit high and mighty, overly concerned about their own purity and not really in touch with the common person. The hearers might be expecting the next man to be the local beloved rabbi, who would surely help the wounded man. This would be a fitting climax to the parable. The bait has been set in this mousetrap (see chap. 3 for parables as mousetraps).

Jesus drops the bombshell: "But a Samaritan, as he traveled, came where the man was; and when he saw him, he took pity on him. He went to him and bandaged his wounds, pouring on oil and wine. Then he put the man on his own donkey, brought him to an inn and took care of him" (Lk 10:33-34). Again, we can't really hear this story the way a Jew would have heard it in the first century. A Samaritan! This was the worst of the worst, the scum of the earth. For a modern American it would be like saying "a drug dealer came along and helped the man," or "a Muslim jihadist came along and paid for his care."

Jesus concludes by asking, "Which of these three do you think was a neighbor to the man who fell into the hands of robbers?" The man apparently can't bring himself to say, "the Samaritan," and so simply replies, "The one who had mercy on him." Jesus concludes, "Go and do likewise" (Lk 10:36-37).

Jesus' point is clear. There is no room for prejudice or hatred in the kingdom of God. A true neighbor, one who fulfills God's command to "love your neighbor as yourself," shows love for all people, whatever their ethnicity or national identity.

An inclusive vision of the kingdom of God. There are other passages that demonstrate Jesus' inclusive vision for the kingdom of God. After healing ten men of leprosy, he commends the one who returns to show gratitude for the healing. Jesus points out that this man is a foreigner, a Samaritan (Lk 17:11-19). On another occasion, he rebukes James and John for their desire to call down fire from heaven on a Samaritan village (Lk 9:52-56).

When Jesus angrily clears the temple of money changers, he explains the reason by quoting Isaiah 56:7, "My house will be called a house of prayer for all nations" (Mt 21:13//Mk 11:17//Lk 19:46). The temple's purpose was to be a place for all people to come and worship God. By selling animals and exchanging money in the outer Court of the Gentiles, the religious leaders were impeding this purpose.

Finally, of course, Jesus gives his disciples the Great Commission. They are to go and make disciples *of all nations* (Mt 28:18-20). They are to proclaim the good news of salvation outward in concentric circles, being his witnesses "in Jerusalem, and in all Judea and Samaria, *and to the ends of the earth*" (Acts 1:8). It is significant that this last phrase echoes Isaiah 49:6—a passage we cited earlier—which says that the role of God's servant Israel is to be "a light for the Gentiles, that my salvation may reach *to the ends of the earth*." Jesus calls on his followers to fulfill God's vision to announce his salvation to all people everywhere.

CONCLUSION

By healing the daughter of the Syrophoenician woman and the centurion's servant, by illustrating his Nazareth sermon with Gentile examples, by telling parables like the good Samaritan, and by commending the gratitude of a foreigner healed of leprosy, Jesus reveals that the heart of his message is for all people everywhere. Although God's plan of salvation entailed choosing Israel as his special people and bringing the Messiah through this line of Abraham, Isaac and Jacob, all along God's purpose was to restore and redeem all nations. Just as Adam's sin affected all people everywhere, so the redemption accomplished through Jesus the Messiah is good news for the whole world.

Sadly, throughout history it has often been those claiming to be Christians who have promoted racism. But anyone who claims the name of Christ should embrace Jesus' own mission for the people of the world. This passion is well illustrated in John's vision of heaven in Revelation 7:9-10:

> After this I looked, and there before me was a great multitude that no one could count, from every nation, tribe, people and language, standing before the throne and before the Lamb. They were wearing white robes and were holding palm branches in their hands. And they cried out in a loud voice:
>
> "Salvation belongs to our God,
> who sits on the throne,
> and to the Lamb."

In the end, people of every nation, tribe, people and language will gather as one choir to worship God before his throne. All who desire to serve God should join that chorus now.

SEXIST OR EGALITARIAN?

IF WE'RE SO EQUAL, WHY DO THE BOYS GET ALL THE GOOD JOBS?

I JUST DON'T LIKE PAUL. He seems angry all the time. And he seems to dislike women." The woman I was speaking with after the service expressed a view that I had heard many times. When discussing the volatile issue of the role of women in the church and the home, the apostle Paul is usually in the crosshairs. After all, Paul is the one who did not allow women to teach or assume authority over men (1 Tim 2:11-12). Paul commanded women to be silent in church (1 Cor 14:34) and to cover their heads in worship (1 Cor 11:5-6). Paul also said wives should submit to their husbands (Eph 5:22; Col 3:18; Tit 2:5). For many modern readers this sounds backward and old-fashioned, a bit like burka-covered women of Islamic fundamentalism. Haven't we moved beyond this barbarism to recognize women as equals?

This is not a book about Paul, and so we will not take a lot of time to defend him. Yet we must note in passing that Paul often gets a bad rap. Though he did make a number of restrictive statements about women, these must be understood in the cultural and historical context in which he lived. The first-century world, and Judaism in particular, was strongly patriarchal, with men taking the lead in public and private life. There is a lively debate among Christians today concerning how much of what Paul says is a condescension to the culture of his day and how much of it is meant for the church of all time. In a patriarchal culture, allowing women to teach or lead men would have been scandalous in certain situations, and Paul seems to be trying to avoid giving the church a bad name.

Indeed, Paul seems remarkably progressive at times. He works closely with women and speaks of them as his "coworkers" in ministry (Rom 16:3 [Priscilla]; Phil 4:2-3 [Euodia and Syntyche]). Priscilla in particular seems to have taken a prominent role in training the preacher Apollos (Acts 18:26) and in coleading house churches in Corinth, Ephesus and Rome (Acts 18:2, 18-19; Rom 16:3). Paul also refers to a woman named Phoebe as a "deacon," apparently a leadership office in the church, and entrusts to her the important task of carrying his magnum opus, the letter to the Romans, to the church in Rome (Rom 16:1). Paul may actually refer to one woman, Junia, as an apostle (Rom 16:7). The meaning and application of these passages are greatly debated, and our purpose here is not to resolve them—that would take a much longer book. The point is that Paul's view of women is certainly not as negative as some make it out to be, and may be seen as progressive in the cultural context he lived in.

Our concern, however, is with Jesus. Jesus is commonly viewed as a great liberator of women and advocate of their rights. As we will see, it is certainly true that he had followers who were women and treated women with respect and honor. Yet with all his counter-cultural tendencies, he still chose twelve *men* to be his apostles, evidently locking women out of the highest positions of authority. Was Jesus sexist?

WOMEN IN FIRST-CENTURY JUDAISM

For the most part, the world of Jesus' day considered women to be inferior to men. Women had few rights and were viewed as the possession of their fathers and their husbands. There is no shortage of statements confirming this. The first-century Jewish historian Josephus wrote, "Scripture says, 'A woman is inferior to her husband in all things.' Let her, therefore, be obedient to him; not so that he should abuse her, but that she may acknowledge her duty to her husband; for God has given the authority to the husband."[1] Josephus does not state *which* Scripture says women are inferior to men, and no statement like this appears in the Hebrew Bible. He is probably referring to a particular rabbinic interpretation of a passage, perhaps the creation account of Genesis 2.

In Judaism women were not viewed as reliable witnesses and were not allowed to give testimony in court.[2] This was because they were viewed as intellectually and morally inferior to men. Philo, the Jewish philosopher from Alexandria, Egypt (c. 25 B.C.–A.D. 50), wrote that "the minds of women are, in some degree, weaker than those of men, and are not so well able to comprehend a thing that is appreciable only by the intellect, without any aid of objects addressed to the outward senses."[3] Eve was primarily to blame for humanity's fall because she was the weak and gullible one. In his commentary on Genesis, Philo asserts that in the Garden of Eden the serpent approached Eve first because "the woman was more accustomed to be deceived than the man . . . and is taken in by plausible falsehoods which resemble the truth."[4] He continues, "The woman, being imperfect and depraved by nature, made the beginning of sinning and prevaricating; but the man, as being the more excellent and perfect creature, was the first to set the example of blushing and of being ashamed, and indeed, of every good feeling and action."[5] I have a feeling Philo would not have fared well on the *Oprah Winfrey Show*.

Though women and girls would hear the Scriptures read during Sabbath synagogue services, they were not formally taught the Jewish law as boys were in synagogue school. Speaking with women about religious matters was considered a waste of time that could be better spent in study of Torah. A proverb from the Jewish Mishnah (c. A.D. 200) quotes "the sages" as saying, "He who talks much with womankind brings evil upon himself and neglects the study of the law and at the last will inherit Gehenna [Hell]."[6]

Though there were no doubt exceptions to such condescending and demeaning attitudes toward women, these statements represent the predominant male attitude of Jesus' day. A famous rabbinic prayer sums up well the perspective of many Jewish men: "Blessed are you, God, for not making me a heathen, a woman, or a slave."[7]

JESUS' AFFIRMATION OF WOMEN

Jesus' attitude toward women stands in striking contrast to this. He was willing to speak openly about theological matters with the Samaritan woman at the well in John 4. He commended the theological insight and persistent faith of the Syrophoenician woman who requested healing for her daughter (Mk 7:24-30//Mt 15:21-28). He praised the poor widow in the temple who generously gave an offering out of her poverty in contrast to the rich who gave only a tiny fraction of their wealth (Mk 12:41-44//Lk 21:1-4). He commended a woman for her great sacrifice and spiritual insight in anointing his head with expensive perfume in preparation for his burial (Mk 14:3-9//Mt 26:6-13; identified as Mary of Bethany in Jn 12:1-8).

Jesus especially showed care and concern for women who were poor, outcast or oppressed. He commended the faith of a woman with a blood disease who was healed when she secretly touched his garment (Mk 5:25-34//Mt 9:20-22//Lk 8:43-48). He spoke of the "great love" shown by the sinful woman who anointed his feet with

oil and washed them with her tears (Lk 7:36-50). He showed compassion to the widow of Nain by raising her only son from the dead
(Lk 7:11-17). He told the parable of the persistent widow to illustrate
what it means to persevere in prayer (Lk 18:1-8). He prevented the
execution of the woman caught in adultery by rebuking the hypocrisy of the bystanders: "Let any one of you who is without sin
be the first to throw a stone at her" (Jn 8:7).

Most surprising of all, Jesus counted women among his disciples,
something unheard of for Jewish rabbis of his day. Mark names a
number of these women and points out that "in Galilee these
women had followed him and cared for his needs" (Mk 15:41). The
language of "following" is the same used of Jesus' male disciples
(e.g., Mt 4:20, 22; 8:10, 19, 22; 9:9; 10:38; 19:21, 27). Luke describes a
number of women of means who supported Jesus' ministry and
traveled with him and his other disciples:

> Jesus traveled about from one town and village to another,
> proclaiming the good news of the kingdom of God. The
> Twelve were with him, and also some women who had been
> cured of evil spirits and diseases: Mary (called Magdalene)
> from whom seven demons had come out; Joanna the wife of
> Chuza, the manager of Herod's household; Susanna; and
> many others. These women were helping to support them out
> of their own means. (Lk 8:1-3)

While there were many interested observers of Jesus' ministry,
we learn here that two main groups were closest to him—the
Twelve and a group of prominent women who helped to support
him financially. These were his most faithful followers. Even when
all his male disciples deserted him at his arrest, these women were
present at the cross (Mk 15:40-41//Mt 27:55-56//Lk 23:49). They
also observed the place where Jesus was buried, visited his tomb on
Sunday morning, and were the first to receive the announcement

of the resurrection (Mk 15:47//Mt 27:61//Lk 23:55; Mk 16:1-8//Mt 28:1-8//Lk 24:1-8).

The most prominent of these women disciples was Mary Magdalene, who is always named first in lists like this (as Peter is in lists of the Twelve male disciples). Though sensationalistic claims made in books like *The Da Vinci Code* that Mary was Jesus' wife or mistress are silly, without any historical basis, Mary *was* clearly an important leader among Jesus' female disciples.[8] Not only does she appear prominently in these lists of followers, but she had the privilege to be the first of his disciples to see the resurrected Lord (Jn 20:14-18). Although Mary has historically been portrayed as a reformed prostitute, there is no historical evidence for this. This false identification is based on confusion between various women named Mary in the New Testament (a very common name) and various women who anointed Jesus' head or feet.[9] Though Mary's age is never stated, she may have been an elderly widow whose husband had left her substantial means, with which she helped to support Jesus' ministry. All we know for sure about her is that Jesus had freed her from demon possession (Lk 8:2).

It is another Mary, however, Mary of Bethany, whose story most clearly illustrates Jesus' attitude toward women. Luke recounts an episode when Jesus visited the home of Martha and her sister Mary (Lk 10:38-42). Though Luke does not tell us so here, their home was in Bethany, near Jerusalem, where the sisters lived with their brother Lazarus (Jn 11:1-42; 12:1-11). Luke relates only that the home was Martha's, and that she was busy with preparations for the meal. Mary, meanwhile, sat at Jesus' feet. The scene itself is culturally surprising, since to "sit at the feet" indicates the position of a disciple (Acts 22:3 ESV, NRSV). As noted earlier, in Judaism it was considered inappropriate for a woman to assume such a role. When Martha objects that Mary has left her with the work, Jesus responds, "Martha, Martha, . . . you are worried and upset about many things, but few things are needed—or indeed only one. Mary has chosen what is better, and it will not be taken away from her" (Lk 10:41-42).

The one thing that is needed is a relationship with Jesus, and more specifically, a position as his disciple, learning from him. Whereas in Judaism it was scandalous for a woman to assume such a role, Jesus praises Mary for doing so. Here we see Jesus breaking down cultural barriers with an inclusive vision of the kingdom of God.

TWELVE (MALE) APOSTLES

If Jesus had such a progressive attitude toward women, what about the twelve male apostles? Why this exclusive club? While the Gospels make it clear Jesus had many followers, he chose twelve to be his core leadership. And these twelve were all men. Mark records their appointment:

> Jesus went up on a mountainside and called to him those he wanted, and they came to him. He appointed twelve that they might be with him and that he might send them out to preach and to have authority to drive out demons. These are the twelve he appointed: Simon (to whom he gave the name Peter), James son of Zebedee and his brother John (to them he gave the name Boanerges, which means "sons of thunder"), Andrew, Philip, Bartholomew, Matthew, Thomas, James son of Alphaeus, Thaddaeus, Simon the Zealot and Judas Iscariot, who betrayed him. (Mk 3:13-19//Mt 10:1-4//Lk 6:12-16; cf. Jn 6:70)

These twelve were designated "apostles" (Mt 10:2; Mk 6:30; Lk 6:13), a term meaning "messenger" or "emissary." Jesus sent them out to expand his ministry of preaching, healing and exorcism (Mt 10:2-16; Mk 6:8-11; Lk 9:2-5). He often singled the Twelve out for special teaching and made it clear they were to be the official guardians of his message. At the Last Supper, only the Twelve are explicitly named as present (Mk 14:17//Mt 26:20//Lk 22:14). As we have seen, the number twelve is likely symbolic, representing the twelve tribes of Israel, and these were meant to symbolize Israel's restoration. Jesus promised that at the establishment of the new world—the consummation of the kingdom of God—they would sit on twelve thrones judging the twelve tribes of Israel (Mt 19:28; Lk 22:30).

Twelve *men* ruling the twelve tribes? This doesn't sound very inclusive. If Jesus were such a great reformer and promoter of women's rights, why this exclusive leadership? Here we come to an issue that continues to divide the church. Because of this debate, I want to present two possible answers to this question. Both are widely (and vociferously) defended in the church today.

*A **complementarian** perspective.* A complementarian is some-one who believes that, while men and women are equal heirs of God's salvation, they have been given distinct roles in the church and the home.[10] Men are called to lead, to provide and to protect, while women are intended to fulfill more supporting and nurturing roles. Although there are a wide variety of perspectives within this general view, for most complementarians women may lead and teach children and other women, but (in general) they are not to teach or exercise authority over men. Most complementarians do not believe these distinctions are intended for public life (business leadership, public office, etc.) but only for the church and the home. The most quoted passage to defend a complementarian perspective is 1 Timothy 2:12, where Paul says, "I do not permit a woman to teach or to assume authority over a man; she must be quiet."

Those who hold a complementarian position claim that Jesus' choice of the Twelve reflects this God-ordained leadership pattern. Like the priesthood in the Old Testament, which was entirely male, senior leadership in the church should be male. It is not surprising, then, that Jesus appointed twelve men to be his apostles. While all believers are disciples ("followers" of Christ) and all believers exercise spiritual gifts in the body of Christ, men are to assume senior leadership roles such as bishop (or overseer), pastor-teacher, elder and deacon.

An egalitarian perspective. An egalitarian is someone who believes that leadership roles in the church and the home should be based on gifting, not gender, and that in the church of Jesus Christ men and women share equally in both status and roles.[11] This is not to say that men and women are not different biologically, socially, emotionally and so on, but these differences do not disqualify anyone from leadership. Indeed, many traditionally "feminine" qualities, such as gentleness, sensitivity and discernment, are excellent and much-needed qualities for leadership.

A key passage to defend an egalitarian perspective is Galatians 3:28, where Paul says, "There is neither Jew nor Gentile, neither slave nor free, nor is there male and female, for you are all one in Christ Jesus." Just as the coming of God's salvation through Jesus Christ eliminates social divisions between slaves and free, and ethnic divisions between Jews and Gentiles, so it extinguishes gender biases. While it is true that the Old Testament ordained a male priesthood, the New Testament teaches the priesthood of *all believers* (1 Pet 2:5, 9), evidence that old distinctions no longer apply. All believers—men and women alike—have equal access to God through the one mediator, Jesus Christ, and so all believers share equally in all of God's gifts and callings.

Those who hold an egalitarian perspective tend to view statements by Paul and others about the subordination of women as culturally conditioned. Paul and Peter encourage wives to submit to their husbands because it would have been socially and culturally inappropriate and disruptive to do otherwise (Eph 5:22-24; Col 3:18; Titus 2:5; 1 Pet 3:1). Yet Paul hints at an egalitarian perspective by encouraging *mutual* submission among believers (Eph 5:21). Most

Christians today acknowledge that Paul's admonition for women to cover their heads in worship or for believers to greet one another with a kiss were culturally specific standards that do not necessarily apply to Christians today. In the same way egalitarians argue that the commands related to male leadership were not intended to be universal and enduring standards, but instead were condescension to first-century cultural norms.

The same would be said about Jesus' choice of the Twelve. It would have been scandalous for Jesus to choose women for his inner circle of disciples, a distraction from his mission to call Israel to repentance and faith in the kingdom of God. There was also the Old Testament precedence of the twelve *sons* of Jacob/Israel forming the twelve tribes.[12] To reflect this reality it was appropriate for Jesus to choose twelve male disciples, without necessarily prescribing future male leadership over the church.

Toward a Solution?

This is a tremendously complex topic, and I cannot hope to solve it in this short section. My own personal views lie somewhere between traditional complementarian and egalitarian positions. I believe God *generally* calls men to leadership roles and women to more supportive roles. But there have been many exceptions to this biblically (e.g., Miriam, Huldah, Deborah, Priscilla, Phoebe, Junia) as well as historically.[13] God can (and does) call whomever he chooses to leadership roles.

Yet from either perspective, Jesus can hardly be called "sexist." He affirmed women in a way that was seldom seen in his day, treating them as disciples and as coheirs of the kingdom of God. Depending on your theology of women and men, his choice of twelve male disciples is either (1) an affirmation of God's intention that men would serve in senior leadership roles in the church, or (2) an example of God's self-revelation in culturally appropriate ways.

Was Jesus
Anti-Semitic?

Shepherd of Israel's Lost Sheep

WHEN MEL GIBSON'S MOVIE *The Passion of the Christ* was released in 2004 it created a firestorm of criticism. Not only was the movie full of graphic violence in its depiction of the last twelve hours of Jesus' life, but critics also claimed it was anti-Semitic, characterizing the Jews as fanatical murderers of Christ. Shortly before the movie's release I remember meeting with a group of Jewish leaders who were deeply disturbed by its content and were concerned that it would increase anti-Jewish feelings in the community.

Anti-Semitism in the Church

Anti-Semitism—hatred for Jews—has been a terrible stain on the history of the church through the centuries. During the Middle Ages, Jewish communities in Europe were often subject to persecution, segregation in ghettos, forced conversion and even murder. In the period of the Crusades, when "Christian" armies headed to the Middle East to free the Holy Land from its Muslim conquerors, the Crusaders often vented their anger first on European Jews.

Thousands were killed. During the Black Death, the horrific bubonic plague that killed over a third of Europe's population in the mid-fourteenth century, the Jews were made scapegoats as rumors spread that they had caused the plague by poisoning wells. In 1348 in the city of Strasbourg alone nine hundred Jews were burned alive. During the Spanish Inquisition of the 1480s and 1490s under King Ferdinand and Queen Isabel, many Jews were expelled from Spain, and anyone suspected of secretly practicing Judaism was subject to arrest, torture and execution.

This is just a small sampling of the persecutions inflicted on the Jews over the centuries. Of course anti-Semitism reached its most horrific climax in the Nazi Holocaust of World War II, when over six million Jews were killed.

Throughout history those seeking to justify their anti-Jewish views have often turned to the New Testament, where the Jewish people are portrayed as responsible in part for Jesus' death. When Pilate asks the crowds of Jerusalem what to do with Jesus, they cry out, "Crucify him!" Pilate pleads Jesus' innocence, but they shout all the more, "Crucify him!" (Mt 27:21-24//Mk 15:12-14//Lk 23:20-23; Jn 19:14-15). Movies often portray Pilate as a reasonable but powerless governor and the Jewish crowds as wild and bloodthirsty. In Matthew's Gospel in particular, Pilate tries to wash his hands (literally) of any role in Jesus' execution, saying, "I am innocent of this man's blood." The people cry out, "His blood is on us and on our children!" (Mt 27:24-25). This line has haunted Jewish and Christian relations ever since. Throughout history Jews were often labeled "Christ killers" and were considered cursed by God because of their actions. Whatever evil befell them was deemed just punishment for what they did to their Messiah.

Even some respected Christian leaders have fallen under the spell of anti-Semitism. Most famous was Martin Luther (1483–1546), whose preaching on salvation by faith alone launched the

Protestant Reformation. Although early in his career Luther expressed concern for the Jews of Europe and hoped for their conversion, late in his life he turned increasingly, and violently, anti-Semitic. In a sermon near the end of his life he said of the Jews,

> They are our public enemies. They do not stop blaspheming our Lord Christ, calling the Virgin Mary a whore, Christ, a bastard. . . . If they could kill us all, they would gladly do it. They do it often, especially those who pose as physicians. . . . They administer poison to someone from which he could die in an hour, a month, a year, ten or twenty years. . . . Therefore, do not be involved with them as with those who do nothing else among you than heinously blaspheme our dear Lord Jesus Christ and deprive us of body, life, honor, and goods.[1]

Luther advocated that the synagogues and schools of the Jews should be burned, prayer books destroyed, rabbis forbidden to preach and property confiscated.[2] Luther's anti-Semitic views were not racial but religious. If Jews would convert, they would be freely accepted into the Christian fold. But Luther's status and authority in Germany certainly contributed to racial prejudice and persecution against the Jews. His incendiary comments were later picked up by those who justified the Nazi Holocaust on racial grounds.

If someone so steeped in the Scriptures as Martin Luther held anti-Semitic views, how far back can these be traced? Was Jesus anti-Semitic?

JESUS AND THE JEWISH LEADERSHIP: JEW VERSUS JEW

As we have seen, Jesus strongly denounced the Pharisees and scribes (see chap. 3). He attacked them for their pride, hypocrisy and opposition to the kingdom of God. He called them a variety of names: hypocrites, blind guides, blind fools, greedy, self-indulgent, murderers, sons of snakes, children of hell. Jesus obviously criti-cized the Jewish leadership of Israel.

Yet to say that Jesus or his earliest followers were anti-Semitic is anachronistic, misrepresenting the historical situation. Jesus was (of course) himself Jewish, and all of his original followers were Jews. The very real conflict we see in the Gospels was not "Jew versus Christian"; it was "Jew versus Jew." Jesus was launching a reform movement *within* Judaism. Or, to put it more precisely, Jesus was claiming that God's purpose and actions through his people, the Jews, was coming to its climax and fulfillment in Jesus' own words and deeds. This is not *anti*-Judaism; it is *pro*-Judaism— an affirmation that Israel was the true people of God, whose role was to bring God's salvation to the world. Jesus called his people to return to faithfulness to their covenant God and to believe that God's promises for salvation were coming to fulfillment.

In fact, the term *the Jews* is never used with reference to Jesus' enemies in the Synoptic Gospels (Matthew, Mark and Luke). In the Synoptics Jesus faces opposition from the *Pharisees* and the *Sadducees*, religious parties within Judaism, and from the *scribes*, experts in the Jewish law, but his opponents are never called "the Jews." The term *Jews* is only used in a neutral ethnic sense in ex-pressions like "king of the Jews" and "elders of the Jews"—never in a derogatory sense.[3] These various groups within Judaism— Pharisees, scribes, Sadducees, Herodians—opposed Jesus because he challenged their authority and threatened their influence with the people.

When we turn to the Gospel of John, however, a very different picture emerges.

THE "JEWS" IN JOHN'S GOSPEL

We should perhaps call this chapter "John Behaving Badly," since the charge of anti-Semitism relates primarily to the presentation of the Jewish people in the Gospel of John. It is John's Gospel that repeatedly refers to Jesus' opponents as "the Jews."

The meaning of "the Jews" in John's Gospel. The Greek word commonly translated "the Jews" (*Ioudaioi*) occurs seventy-one times in John's Gospel. Though some Bible versions consistently translate this word as "the Jews," it is clear in many contexts that it has a more specific meaning. For example, when some people in Jerusalem (all Jews) say that Jesus is a good man, the narrator tells us that they wouldn't say so publicly "for fear of the Jews" (Jn 7:13 NRSV). It is strange to hear that the Jews were afraid of the Jews!

Similarly, we learn that the parents of the blind man Jesus healed in John 9 would not disclose how he was healed "because they were afraid of the Jews; for the Jews had already agreed that anyone who confessed Jesus to be the Messiah would be put out of the synagogue" (Jn 9:22 NRSV). The parents, who are themselves Jewish, are afraid of "the Jews"? In John 19 we learn that Joseph of Arimathea, who himself was a Jewish leader, was a secret follower of Jesus "because of his fear of the Jews" (Jn 19:38 NRSV). In all these cases it is clear that "the Jews" refers not to the Jewish people in general but to those Jewish leaders who stood in opposition to Jesus. Of course Jesus and his disciples are also Jewish, so whenever we learn that "the Jews" opposed him, this must mean a very specific group who disliked his activities.

While the more formal Bible versions translate *Ioudaioi* consistently as "the Jews" (e.g., NRSV, NASB, NKJV, ESV) other more idiomatic versions translate according to the specific meaning in context. For example, in John 7:13 the NIV translates that the people in Jerusalem kept their thoughts about Jesus quiet "for fear of the leaders" rather than "for fear of the Jews." The parents of the man healed of blindness were afraid of "the Jewish leaders" (NIV, NLT, NET) rather than simply afraid of "the Jews" (NRSV, NASB, NKJV, ESV). And Joseph of Arimathea remained a secret disciple because he feared "the Jewish leaders" (NIV, NLT, NET). In other contexts the word clearly means "the Jews" generally, as when John speaks of the "Passover of the Jews" (Jn 2:13; 6:4; 11:55 NRSV) or when Jesus tells the Samaritan woman at the well that "salvation is from the Jews" (Jn 4:22).

Is John anti-Semitic? The time and circumstances of John's Gospel. While it is clear that John uses the Greek term in two different ways, both with reference to the Jews generally and to the Jewish religious leaders, this does not explain why he uses it so frequently with reference to Jesus' opponents. This is especially surprising since the Synoptics never use it this way. The answer is almost certainly that John is writing at a different time and under different circumstances than the other three Gospels

John's Gospel was evidently written late in the first century, when Jews and Christians had mostly parted ways and Christianity was being viewed as a separate religion. The early Christians—who called themselves followers of "the Way"—had no intention to create a new religion. They viewed their faith as the fulfillment of Judaism and themselves as followers of the Jewish Messiah. The church, made up of Jews and Gentiles, represented the end-time people of God, and the Hebrew Scriptures (the Old Testament) constituted their Bible.

By the time John wrote, however, the church and the synagogue had experienced a serious breach and were rapidly becoming two distinct religions. What was once a conflict between two Jewish groups—those who believed Jesus was the Messiah and those who did not—was now a struggle between "Jews" and "Christians." While John, like the Synoptics, still refers frequently to the "Pharisees" as Jesus' opponents, he more often refers to these opponents simply as "the Jews." In this way he is projecting language from his own time and place onto Jesus' ministry.

"Anti-Semitism" as anachronistic. So was the author of the Fourth

Gospel anti-Semitic by referring to Jesus' opponents as "the Jews"?
Throughout John's Gospel, Jesus is at odds with "the Jews." While they
claim to be Abraham's children, he says they are children of the devil—
a liar and a murderer (Jn 8:31-47). They claim to see, but they are actually blind (Jn 9:41). They are supposed to be shepherds tending
God's flock, but he says they are actually thieves, robbers and hired
hands, who abandon the sheep at the first sign of trouble (Jn 10:8-13).

While the author of John's Gospel and his community are clearly
in an antagonistic relationship with the larger Jewish community, it
is again anachronistic to label this "anti-Semitism." Anti-Semitism
refers to prejudice and antagonism against a minority group, who are
viewed as inferior to those of the majority culture. In John's day the
Christians and the Jews were *both* minority groups seeking to win
supporters and trying to survive in an often hostile Greco-Roman
culture. They are in conflict with one another because both claim to
be the authentic followers of the one true God of Israel. Both claim
the Hebrew Scriptures apply to them. Both are competing to establish strong relationships with Gentile patrons who will support
and defend them in the cities throughout the Roman Empire.

This sometimes violent struggle is evident in the book of Acts, as
Paul and other missionaries move from synagogue to synagogue
and city to city preaching the message of Jesus. While a small
number of Jews believe, a larger number of Gentile "God fearers"
accept the gospel message. This often provokes a hostile reaction
from the Jewish community, since the Christian missionaries are
viewed as drawing away the synagogue's friends and supporters.
Paul often faces a conflict as his Jewish opponents bring charges
against him before the authorities and try to force him out of town.[4]
In his own writings Paul speaks of being whipped by "the Jews" on
five different occasions with forty lashes (2 Cor 11:24). These episodes were no doubt punishments sanctioned by synagogue leaders
as a result of Paul's preaching.

From the perspective of the Jewish community, Paul was a false prophet leading their people astray. He is sheep stealing—robbing them of their converts and supporters. It was essential to protect their relational investment. A modern parallel might be if a Christian cult moved into your area and began to convince members of your church to join them. From their perspective they are the true people of God. From your perspective they are heretics practicing a false religion. Your church leadership would surely be concerned and would take steps to oppose and refute them.

It should be obvious that this conflict between small communities of Jesus-followers and the larger Jewish community can hardly be called anti-Semitism. It is rather an internecine struggle between two sects within Judaism, each trying to assert itself as the true people of God.

We have early evidence of this struggle between Jews and Christians in the larger Roman world. The Roman historian Suetonius, writing around A.D. 120, describes how Emperor Claudius expelled the Jews from Rome in A.D. 49 because of "of continuous disturbances at the instigation of Chrestus."[5] This same expulsion is mentioned by Luke in Acts 18:2. Most scholars consider "Chrestus" mentioned by Suetonius to be a misspelling of the word "Christ" (*Christos*). Suetonius evidently thought that Chrestus was a ringleader of the group. In reality, Jews and Jewish Christians in Rome were in conflict over the question of whether Jesus was "the Christ" (i.e., the Messiah). The continuous violence between the two groups provoked Claudius to expel *all Jews* from Rome, since he could not distinguish between the two.

CONCLUSION: READING THE BIBLE IN CONTEXT

The conflict between Jesus and "the Jews" in John's Gospel is an important reminder to read the whole Bible (and all literature) in the context in which it was written. Rather than an example of anti-

Semitism, John's presentation is a reminder of the turbulent cultural context in which Christianity was born. It is also a reminder of the importance of the Jewish background and context in which the message of Jesus and the early church arose.

FAILED PROPHET
OR VICTORIOUS KING?

DOOMSDAY PROPHET OF
THE END OF THE WORLD?

THE END OF THE WORLD IS HERE!" Throughout history
many people have predicted the soon end of the world. In the early
1800s William Miller, a Baptist preacher and self-proclaimed
prophecy expert, developed a system of Bible interpretation that
he claimed would let him predict the return of Christ and the end
of the world. Scores of people—known as Millerites—followed
him. He first predicted a date for the return of Christ between
March 21, 1843, and March 21, 1844. When this date came and
went, one of his followers refined his method and came up with a
new date—October 22, 1844! Some Millerites even sold their
property and possessions as they awaited this momentous event.
When the day passed without incident, their faith was shattered.
The event became known in history as "The Great Disappointment."[1]

Miller wasn't the first or the last to predict the end of the world.
Apocalyptic sages can be found in almost every age.[2] Take the Es-
senes of Qumran, the Jewish sect that produced the Dead Sea
Scrolls. They holed up in their remote community in the Judean

desert expecting the Messiah to arrive any day and lead them to victory against the Romans. The *War Scroll* even provides troop formations and battle plans. Then there were the Montanists, a charismatic sect of the second century A.D. named after its founder, Montanus. The Montanists believed Christ would shortly return to Phrygia in Asia Minor and there set up the New Jerusalem. Hippolytus of Rome (A.D. 170–235) did even better, calculating the return of Christ precisely to the year A.D. 500.

In more recent times there are the Jehovah's Witnesses, who predicted multiple dates for Christ's return, first in 1914, then 1915, 1918, 1920, 1925, 1941, 1975 and 1994. Finally, they decided that Christ did in fact return in 1914, but that it was a secret return (very convenient!). Just a few years ago Harold Camping, radio broadcaster and evangelist, claimed that, by his calculations, Jesus Christ would return on May 21, 2011. Using his significant fortune, Camping and his company, Family Radio, purchased billboards all over America, trumpeting "Judgment Day, May 21." Needless to say, judgment day was again a bust.

The next year saw another outbreak of end-time fever. This time it was not Christian but Mayan. The ancient Mayan "long calendar" apparently came to an end December 21, 2012, heralding the end of time as we know it. Pundits and cartoonists had a heyday. One of my favorite cartoons shows a Mayan sitting at a bar looking depressed. The bartender, seeking to console him, says, "Cheer up, it's not the end of the world." Alas, he was right. Most real Mayan experts denied the calendar ever predicted the end of the world. Instead it simply indicated the end of one calendar cycle and the beginning of another.

We tend to think of people who predict the end of the world as a bit unbalanced. There is that iconic picture of the wild-eyed guy with the disheveled beard and the sandwich board proclaiming, "The End of the World Is Here!" While these prophets of doom may gather some loyal (and gullible?) supporters, these followers usually disperse or find other kooky causes when things don't work out as predicted.

But wait a minute. Didn't all this start with Jesus himself? Didn't he predict the soon end of the world? Didn't he announce that the kingdom of God "has come near" (Mk 1:14-15//Mt 4:17)? Didn't he say the Son of Man would come on the clouds of heaven and that this would happen within a generation (Mk 13:26-30//Mt 24:30-34// Lk 21:27-32)? Didn't he say the stars would soon fall from the sky and the sun and the moon disappear (Mk 13:24-25//Mt 24:29)? Didn't he say that some of those with him would not die until they saw the kingdom of God arrive with power (Mk 9:1//Mt 19:28//Lk 9:27)? Didn't his first followers believe he would return within their lifetime (1 Thess 4:16-17)? Was Jesus a doomsday prophet whose crazy predictions just didn't pan out?

Throughout this book we have been looking at some of the really hard sayings and actions of Jesus. But most scholars—even the most liberal ones—do *not* see Jesus as a warmongering, hate-filled, legalistic, ethnocentric, misogynist, anti-Semitic, crazy man. At the same time, neither do they view him as the Son of God and Savior of the world. From their perspective the Jesus of history was a Jewish prophet who sought to call Israel to repentance in light of *the soon end of the world*—the kingdom of God. But instead of bringing in God's final salvation, he became a victim of the politics of his day. After causing a disturbance of some kind in the temple in Jerusalem, he was arrested, condemned and crucified by the Roman authorities. End of story. In short, Jesus—like so many others before and since—was a *failed* end-times prophet.

In *The Quest of the Historical Jesus*, Albert Schweitzer (1875–1965) claimed that Jesus was just this sort of apocalyptic prophet, expecting the soon end of the world. Schweitzer thought that at first Jesus did not view himself as the Messiah. He believed that

God would soon send the "Son of Man," a heavenly messianic figure spoken about in the prophecies of Daniel, who would destroy the enemies of God and establish his kingdom. Yet when this Son of Man did not show up as expected, Jesus changed his perspective. He concluded that he himself must become the Son of Man. By going to Jerusalem and challenging the authorities, he would provoke God to act on his behalf. Here is Schweitzer's famous conclusion:

> Jesus . . . in the knowledge that He is the coming Son of Man lays hold of the wheel of the world to set it moving on that last revolution which is to bring all ordinary history to a close. It refuses to turn, and He throws Himself upon it. Then it does turn; and crushes Him. Instead of bringing in the eschatological conditions, He has destroyed them. The wheel rolls onward, and the mangled body of the one immeasurably great Man, who was strong enough to think of Himself as the spiritual ruler of mankind and to bend history to His purpose, is hanging upon it still. That is His victory and His reign.[3]

For Schweitzer, Jesus was a tragic victim of his own false hopes and aspirations, although he did find a measure of greatness in Jesus as a human leader.

While few scholars agree with Schweitzer's entire proposal, many view Jesus as an end-times prophet. Bart Ehrman, like Schweitzer, views Jesus as a failed apocalyptic prophet. He writes,

> The historical Jesus did not teach about his own divinity or pass on to his disciples the doctrines that later came to be embodied in the Nicene Creed. His concerns were those of a first-century Jewish apocalypticist. Jesus anticipated that the end of the age was coming within his own generation. God would soon send a cosmic judge from heaven to right all the wrongs of this world,

to overthrow the wicked and oppressive powers that opposed both God and his people, to bring in a perfect kingdom in which there would be no more hatred, war, disease, calamity, despair, sin, or death. People needed to repent in view of this coming day of judgment, for it was almost here.[4]

According to Ehrman, things did not work out as Jesus expected. He came to Jerusalem and made some kind of play for power, probably by causing a disturbance in the temple. He was arrested and turned over to Pilate, who had him summarily executed.

So, was Jesus a failed prophet or was he Israel's Messiah and Savior of the world? Was his death just one more act of brutality meted out by Roman thugs, or was it an atoning sacrifice that paid for the sins of the world and launched the new age of salvation? These are radically different options! We might say that the ultimate "bad behavior" for Jesus would be if his expectations for the coming of God's kingdom turned out to be wrong and his life's mission was a grand failure. To address this issue we have to return to two key questions that we have touched on earlier: What is the kingdom of God, and how did Jesus expect it to arrive?

WHAT IS THE KINGDOM OF GOD?

Pretty much everyone agrees that Jesus' central message concerned the "kingdom of God" (Mk 1:14-15). But what was the nature of this kingdom? At its essence, the kingdom of God refers to God's authority and dominion, his sovereign rule over the universe. He always has been and always will be the sovereign Lord of all. Psalm 145:13 says, "Your kingdom is an everlasting kingdom, / and your dominion endures through all generations." Isaiah 37:16 similarly asserts, "LORD Almighty, the God of Israel, enthroned between the cherubim, you alone are God over all the kingdoms of the earth. You have made heaven and earth."

Yet anyone looking around at this world knows that God's kingdom has been compromised. The world is far from a perfect place. There is evil, hatred, murder, death and calamity all around us. The Bible explains this as a result of human sin. Human beings rejected God's sovereignty, resulting in a broken relationship and the fallen state of all of creation. The Bible's overarching narrative is about God's plan to bring humanity back into a right relationship with him and to restore his reign and kingdom. The Old Testament prophets speak of a day when God's kingdom will again be fully manifested on earth as it is in heaven, when

> the LORD Almighty will reign
>> on Mount Zion and in Jerusalem,
>> and before its elders—with great glory. (Is 24:23)

When Jesus announced, "The kingdom of God is at hand," he was referring to this eschatological (end-time) kingdom. But what form would it take, and how would it be established?

WHEN AND HOW DOES THE KINGDOM COME?

Many scholars assume that Jesus expected a cataclysmic intervention by God to establish his kingdom on earth. Since this apparently didn't happen, Jesus must have been wrong. Yet Jesus' own words and actions suggest a more complex picture. In Jesus' teaching and throughout the New Testament, the arrival of God's kingdom is connected to various events: (1) Jesus' public ministry of teaching and miracles, (2) his sacrificial death on the cross, (3) his resurrection as the beginning of the end-time resurrection, (4) his exaltation to the right hand of God and pouring out of the Spirit, (5) the worldwide proclamation of the gospel, (6) the destruction of the temple and the end of the Old Testament sacrificial system, and (7) the return of the Son of Man to consummate the kingdom. In short, the kingdom arrives through the entire "Jesus event"—his life, death, resurrection, ascension and glorious coming to judge and to save. We will briefly survey each of these.

Through Jesus' exorcisms and healings. As we have seen in chapter two, Jesus' understanding of the kingdom is illuminated through the miracles that accompanied his teaching. Jesus healed the sick, cast out demons, raised the dead and exercised authority over nature. None of these point to a defeat of the Roman legions. They all indicate something much greater—the ultimate restoration of creation from its fallen state.

Jesus claimed his exorcisms were evidence of the ultimate defeat of Satan (Lk 10:17-18). By casting out demons he was invading the kingdom of Satan and freeing captives, rescuing them for the kingdom of God. He said, "If it is by the Spirit of God that I drive out demons, then the kingdom of God has come upon you" (Mt 12:28//Lk 11:20).

Jesus' healings were also proof of the coming restoration of creation. When John the Baptist sent his disciples to question whether Jesus was "the One" (i.e., the Messiah), Jesus responded by referring to his miracles and his message: "The blind receive sight, the lame walk, those who have leprosy are cleansed, the deaf hear, the dead are raised, and the good news is proclaimed to the poor" (Lk 7:22//Mt 11:5). Jesus' answer here alludes to various passages in Isaiah concerning God's end-time restoration (Is 26:19; 29:18-21; 35:5-6; 61:1).

This shows that Jesus did not see his ministry as a revolutionary action against Rome or even as a reformation movement within Judaism. By quoting Isaiah's vision of eschatological salvation, Jesus affirms that through him God is launching a rescue plan to renew and restore creation. Consider these passages, where Isaiah envisions the day when all of creation will be made new:

> Then will the eyes of the blind be opened
>   and the ears of the deaf unstopped.

Then will the lame leap like a deer,
    and the mute tongue shout for joy.
Water will gush forth in the wilderness
    and streams in the desert. (Is 35:5-6)

The wolf will live with the lamb,
    the leopard will lie down with the goat,
the calf and the lion and the yearling together;
    and a little child will lead them. . . .
They will neither harm nor destroy
    on all my holy mountain,
for the earth will be filled with the knowledge of the LORD
    as the waters cover the sea. (Is 11:6, 9)

On this mountain he will destroy
    the shroud that enfolds all peoples,
the sheet that covers all nations;
    he will swallow up death forever.
The Sovereign LORD will wipe away the tears
    from all faces. (Is 25:7-8)

No more killing. No more sorrow. No more disease. No more death. Intimate knowledge of God. This is a return to the perfection of Eden. When Jesus quotes Isaiah 35:5-6 to interpret his miracles, he is tapping into Isaiah's vision of eschatological renewal. The kingdom, for Jesus, meant that all of humanity and all of creation would once again be in harmony with God's sovereign rule.

But how was Jesus' vision to be accomplished? While Jesus' contemporaries expected a conquering Messiah to come and make toast of some Roman legions, Jesus kept talking about his own death.

Through Jesus' death as an atoning sacrifice for sins. A decisive turning point takes place in Jesus' ministry after Peter's confession (Mk 8:27-30//Mt 16:13-20//Lk 9:18-21), as Jesus repeatedly predicts his coming death: "He then began to teach them that the Son of Man must suffer many things and be rejected by the elders, the chief priests and the teachers of the law, and that he must be killed and after three days rise again" (Mk 8:31; cf. Mk 9:31; 10:33).

Some scholars consider these so-called "passion predictions" to be creations of the early church, developed after the fact to give meaning to Jesus' death. It is assumed that Jesus could not have predicted his own death. Yet even if we address this issue from a merely human perspective, there is good evidence that Jesus came to Jerusalem expecting and even intending to die.

First, Jesus faced constant opposition and criticism with the religious leaders. They accused him of being a false prophet, breaking the Sabbath, casting out demons by Satan's power, and blasphemy.[5] All of these could be viewed as capital offenses in Judaism. Jesus must have known that his life was in danger. Second, Jesus repeatedly referred to the suffering fate of God's prophets and identified himself as one of them.[6] In his hometown of Nazareth he said that "no prophet is accepted in his hometown" (Lk 4:24). He explained his intention to go to Jerusalem as fulfilling the role of the prophet: "I must press on today and tomorrow and the next day—for surely no prophet can die outside Jerusalem!" (Lk 13:33). It is unlikely that the early church invented sayings in which Jesus referred to himself as a prophet, since they preferred more exalted titles like "Messiah," "Lord" and "Son of God." The evidence suggests Jesus headed for Jerusalem expecting and even intending to die.

So what significance did he give to his impending death? Was he going to Jerusalem to die as a martyr, or was it something more? On only a few occasions does Jesus talk about the *significance* of his coming death. The most important is at the Last Supper.

Almost all scholars today acknowledge that Jesus shared a last meal with his disciples (the Last Supper), during which he instituted a ritual meal (the Lord's Supper) that the church continued to practice after him. The institution of the Lord's Supper is recorded not only in all three Synoptic Gospels but also independently by Paul in 1 Corinthians 11. First Corinthians was written in the mid-50s of the first century, and Paul says that he received this tradition from others before him (1 Cor 11:23). This confirms that we are dealing with very old tradition, likely going back to Jesus himself.

What did Jesus say at this meal? The so-called eucharistic words of Jesus vary slightly in the different sources. The accounts in Matthew and Mark are very similar, as are the accounts in Luke and Paul. In Matthew and Mark, Jesus breaks the bread and says, "Take it; this is my body" (Mk 14:22; cf. Mt 26:26). He then takes the cup and says, "This is my blood of the covenant, which is poured out for many" (Mk 14:24). Matthew's account adds, "for the forgiveness of sins" (Mt 26:28). In Luke and Paul, Jesus distributes the bread and says, "This is my body given for you; do this in re-membrance of me." He then takes the cup and says, "This cup is the new covenant in my blood, which is poured out for you" (Lk 22:19-20; cf. 1 Cor 11:24-25).

Though the words vary somewhat, the essential message is the same. Jesus refers to his coming death as a sacrifice given for others. The shedding of his blood will establish a new covenant with God. The phrase *for many*, which appears in Matthew and Mark, recalls the picture of the suffering servant in Isaiah 53, where "my righteous servant will justify many, and he will bear their iniquities" (Is 53:11). It also recalls Mark 10:45 (//Mt 20:28), where Jesus says, "The Son of Man did not come to be served, but to serve, and to give his life as a ransom for many."

Scholars vigorously debate whether the historical Jesus iden-tified himself with the suffering Servant of Isaiah 53, who gives his life as an atoning sacrifice for his people. But even if we set that question aside for the moment, Jesus' words at the Last Supper carry profound significance. Passover was a national celebration of the exodus, God's deliverance from slavery in Egypt. God brought the nation out of Egypt to Mount Sinai and established his covenant with them, a covenant sealed through blood sacrifices (Ex 19–20).

Jesus now celebrates Passover with his disciples. But, shockingly, he radically revises its meaning, *identifying his own body and blood as the sacrifice that accomplishes a new exodus deliverance and inaugurates the new covenant.* The term *new covenant* used in Luke 22:20 and 1 Corinthians 11:25 alludes to the promise of Jeremiah that God would one day establish a new covenant with his people, bringing true knowledge of God, the law written on their hearts and true forgiveness of sins (Jer 31:31-34). This is a promise for the coming kingdom of God.

This is a truly amazing claim! Jesus is not just calling for the nation Israel to repent of its sins or to purify itself for Passover. He is announcing a radical transformation of the meaning of Passover. This is more than renewal; it is *fulfillment*—the arrival of God's final salvation through the promised new covenant. Since it was God who established the first Passover, Jesus is claiming God's authority to fulfill and transform it.

When Jesus' words here are placed in the framework of his overall ministry, a cohesive picture emerges. Jesus launches his ministry by announcing the kingdom of God. His healings, exorcisms and other miracles are not just deeds of compassion; they are snapshots of the kingdom of God. They preview the defeat of Satan, the reversal of the curse on fallen humanity and the restoration of creation.

But how will this restoration be accomplished? After announcing the kingdom throughout Galilee, Jesus expresses his intention to go to Jerusalem, and speaks of his impending death as an atoning sacrifice (Mk 10:45//Mt 20:28). The eucharistic words at the Last Supper confirm that Jesus viewed his death as a sacrifice for sins, which would initiate a new Passover and a new exodus, establishing a new covenant between God and his people.

So whereas skeptics view Jesus' death as sure evidence that his vision for the kingdom failed, Jesus himself identified it as the *means* by which the kingdom would be established.

Of course *claiming* to be God's agent of salvation and actually being it are two different things. As we have seen, Israel had a history of would-be redeemers and saviors who claimed they were going to lead the nation to victory and deliverance. Yet they came to nothing (see Acts 5:36-38). Jesus claimed that after suffering he would be vindicated by God and rise from the dead. The resurrection is the third stage in the inauguration of the kingdom of God.

Through Jesus' resurrection, the "firstfruits" of the final resurrection. In the Old Testament there are hints of continuing life with God and the ultimate victory over death, but a theology of the resurrection is not well developed there.[7] Only in Daniel 12 is the resurrection explicitly described:

> But at that time your people—everyone whose name is found written in the book—will be delivered. Multitudes who sleep in the dust of the earth will awake: some to everlasting life, others to shame and everlasting contempt. Those who are wise will shine like the brightness of the heavens, and those who lead many to righteousness, like the stars for ever and ever. (Dan 12:1-3)

It is important to understand that in Jewish thought the resurrection was not something that happened within time. It happened *at the end of time*. It was inseparably linked to the final judgment and establishment of the kingdom of God.

Jesus' resurrection was therefore much more than the vindication of his claims (though it was that). If, as I have argued, Jesus viewed his death as the inauguration of the kingdom of God and the promised new covenant (Jer 31), then his resurrection must be viewed as *the beginning of the end-time resurrection of the people of God.* This was not just the restoration of mortal life but the beginning of glorification to a new mode of existence, when God's people would live forever with him and would "shine like the brightness of the heavens" (Dan 12:3).

This is how the apostle Paul understands Jesus' resurrection. Jesus arose in a glorified, immortal and imperishable body, a new mode of existence (1 Cor 15:42-44). In this glorified body, Jesus has become "the firstborn from among the dead" (Col 1:18) and "the firstfruits" of those who have died (1 Cor 15:20). Just as the first part of the harvest is the guarantee of more to come, so Jesus' resurrection is the beginning and guarantee of the final resurrection of all believers. It serves as assurance that they too will be raised to immortal, imperishable resurrection life (1 Cor 15:50-56). In this sense, Jesus' resurrection is the inauguration of God's kingdom.

Through the exaltation of Jesus and the pouring out of the Holy Spirit. Closely linked to the resurrection of Jesus is his exaltation to the right hand of God, from where he pours out the Spirit. According to the Old Testament prophets, a great outpouring of God's Spirit would mark the coming age of salvation (i.e., the kingdom of God). In an eschatological context Isaiah 44:3 reads, "I will pour out my Spirit on your offspring, / and my blessing on your descendants" (see also Is 32:15; Jer 31:31-34; Ezek 39:29). On the day of Pentecost, Peter quotes Joel 2:28-32 to show that the outpouring of the Spirit is the fulfillment of Scripture and the beginning of the end times:

> This is what was spoken by the prophet Joel:
> "In the last days, God says,
> I will pour out my Spirit on all people.
> Your sons and daughters will prophesy,

> your young men will see visions,
> your old men will dream dreams.
> Even on my servants, both men and women,
>   I will pour out my Spirit in those days,
>   and they will prophesy.
> I will show wonders in the heavens above
>   and signs on the earth below,
>   blood and fire and billows of smoke.
> The sun will be turned to darkness
>   and the moon to blood
>   before the coming of the great and glorious day of
>   the Lord.
> And everyone who calls
>   on the name of the Lord will be saved." (Acts 2:16-21)

The cosmic signs in the heavens described here are common in apocalyptic literature, confirming that this is an eschatological event.[8] Yet Peter claims that this event is coming to fulfillment *in the present* with Jesus' resurrection and his ascension to heaven. At the climax of his Pentecost sermon Peter says, "Exalted to the right hand of God, [Jesus] has received from the Father the promised Holy Spirit and has poured out what you now see and hear" (Acts 2:33). God's kingdom is arriving through the outpouring of the Spirit.

The coming of the kingdom at Jesus' exaltation also helps to explain the close connection between the establishment of the kingdom and the "coming" of the Son of Man. The key background passage for Jesus' use of the Son of Man title is Daniel 7:13-14, where the Son of Man comes with the clouds of heaven. In its original context, however, the Son of Man does not come to earth. Daniel writes,

> In my vision at night I looked, and there before me was one like a son of man, coming with the clouds of heaven. He approached the Ancient of Days and was led into his presence.

He was given authority, glory and sovereign power; all nations
and peoples of every language worshiped him. His dominion
is an everlasting dominion that will not pass away, and his
kingdom is one that will never be destroyed. (Dan 7:13-14)

In this passage the coming of the Son of Man is not to earth but
to the presence of God in heaven, where he is vindicated and given
all authority and power. If we ask when Jesus received this authority,
the most obvious answers are at his resurrection (Mt 28:18) and at
this exaltation to the right hand of God (Acts 2:32-36). While the
ultimate fulfillment of this prophecy will be at the second coming,
when the kingdom will be fully established, its initial fulfillment is
his vindication after suffering.

Through the worldwide proclamation of the gospel. Jesus was
not the only one to preach the kingdom of God. Throughout the
book of Acts, the apostles' preaching about Jesus is repeatedly identified as proclaiming "the kingdom of God." Philip preaches the
"good news of the kingdom of God" to the people of Samaria (Acts
8:12). Paul boldly proclaims the kingdom of God during his missionary journeys (Acts 19:8; 28:23). At the climax of Acts, Luke relates that, despite Paul's house arrest, "He proclaimed the kingdom
of God and taught about the Lord Jesus Christ—with all boldness
and without hindrance!" (Acts 28:31). In these contexts the kingdom
of God clearly refers to the salvation that has come through the life,
death, resurrection and ascension of Jesus the Messiah.

This too is in line with Old Testament expectations. Isaiah predicts that the end-time salvation brought by the Servant Messiah
would be "a light for the Gentiles, / that my salvation may reach to
the ends of the earth" (Is 49:6; cf. Is 42:6). The book of Acts presents
the worldwide evangelization by the church as the fulfillment of
these promises. In Acts 1:8 Jesus says that his disciples are to be his
witnesses "in Jerusalem, and in all Judea and Samaria, and *to the*

ends of the earth," alluding to Isaiah 49:6. Paul quotes this same passage in his synagogue sermon in Pisidian Antioch, to show that God has sent him to preach to the Gentiles (Acts 13:47). James quotes Amos 9:11-12 to show that through Jesus the fallen dynasty of David has been restored, so that "the rest of mankind may seek the Lord, / even all the Gentiles who bear my name" (Acts 15:16-17). The kingdom is established through the worldwide proclamation of the gospel.

These passages also confirm another important truth. The church—the people of God in the present age—is not the same as the kingdom of God. It is rather the vehicle God is using to announce and establish his reign in the new age of salvation. As people repent and believe in the salvation accomplished through the life, death and resurrection of Jesus, they submit to God's reign and so enter his kingdom.

At the second coming of Christ, the consummation of salvation. Though the end-time kingdom of God was inaugurated with the life, death, resurrection and ascension of Jesus, it will be consummated when Jesus returns to earth to judge and to save. Jesus said that at the end of the age the Son of Man would send his angels to weed out of his kingdom everything that causes sin and all who do evil. "Then the righteous will shine like the sun in the kingdom of their Father" (Mt 13:40-43). In Matthew 16:27 Jesus says, "the Son of Man is going to come in his Father's glory with his angels, and then he will reward each person according to what they have done" (cf. Mk 8:38//Lk 9:26). This is the final judgment (cf. Mt 25:31-46). Throughout the New Testament the "coming" (*parousia*) of the Lord is associated with Christ's return and the end of the age (1 Thess 3:13; Jas 5:7-8; 2 Pet 1:16; 1 Jn 2:28).[9] These passages clearly point to a final cataclysmic event when the kingdom will come fully and completely on earth.

At the destruction of Jerusalem and the temple. We must add one more event to this discussion of the arrival of the kingdom of God. This is the most controversial and debated of the manifestations of the kingdom discussed here. In his discourse on the Mount of Olives (Mk 13:1-37//Mt 24:1-51//Lk 21:5-36) Jesus links the coming destruction of Jerusalem closely with the establishment of the kingdom of God and the return of the Son of Man. There is good reason for this. With the establishment of the new covenant through the sacrificial death of Christ, the old covenant sacrifices were no longer necessary. As the writer to the Hebrews describes it, the once-for-all death of Christ replaces the temporary and preparatory sacrifices of the old covenant (Heb 8–10).

For the early Christians the destruction of Jerusalem and the temple in A.D. 70 served as, first, judgment against Israel's leaders for rejecting their Messiah, and, second, confirmation that the old covenant sacrifices were at an end because of Christ's atoning sacrifice for sins. In this sense the Son of Man came in judgment, and the kingdom arrived when the old covenant sacrificial system ceased.

In summary, the coming of the kingdom of God relates in its broadest sense to the restoration of humanity to a right relationship with God. It arrives not through any single event but through the entire Jesus event—his life, death, resurrection, exaltation, and return to judge and to save. During Jesus' public ministry he announced the kingdom was arriving through his healings and exorcisms because these were previews or snapshots of the full restoration of creation. The kingdom arrived through his sacrificial death on the cross, which initiated a new Passover and new covenant through his blood. The kingdom arrived with Jesus' resurrection, which signaled the defeat of death and represented the firstfruits of the final resurrection. It was established through the exaltation of Jesus to the right hand of God and his pouring out of the Spirit on the day of Pentecost, which fulfilled the end-time promise for the coming of the Holy Spirit. And it is gradually being established through the proclamation of the gospel to all nations. Its arrival was confirmed through the destruction of Jerusalem in A.D. 70, which verified the end of the old covenant sacrificial system and the fulfillment of the law. Finally, the kingdom of God will be consummated at the second coming of Christ, when the kingdom will come fully, "on earth as it is in heaven" (Mt 6:10).

FOUR DIFFICULT PASSAGES

Having described the various phases of the kingdom's arrival, we turn to four difficult passages that are sometimes said to assert that Jesus was mistaken in his expectations concerning the kingdom.

"You will not finish going through the towns of Israel before the Son of Man comes." The first of these passages occurs only in Matthew's Gospel, when Jesus is instructing the Twelve for their preaching tour of Galilee. In the midst of his instructions he says, "When you are persecuted in one place, flee to another. Truly I tell you, you will not finish going through the towns of Israel before the Son of Man comes" (Mt 10:23). Since the coming of the Son of Man is closely connected to the arrival of the kingdom of God (Mt 13:40-43; 25:31; Mt 16:28//Mk 9:1//Lk 9:27), Jesus seems to be saying that the kingdom will arrive in the near future, before the gospel has been proclaimed throughout Israel.

What is Jesus referring to? In light of the previous discussion, there are various possibilities: (1) the resurrection of Jesus, (2) his exaltation and the coming of the Spirit at Pentecost, (3) the destruction of Jerusalem, or (4) the second coming. On closer examination it is clear that Jesus' teaching in Matthew 10 has two parts. Verses 1-15 concern the immediate situation, the mission of the Twelve in Galilee during Jesus' public ministry. Verses 16-23, however, envision the missionary activity of the disciples after Jesus' resurrection. Jesus tells the disciples in verses 5-6 to go only to the people of Israel, but in verse 18 he speaks of their testifying "before governors and kings as witnesses to them and to the Gentiles." Jesus will not command his disciples to go to the Gentiles in Matthew until the Great Commission, after his resurrection (Mt 28:18-20). So the passage envisions a time after the resurrection when the Gentile mission has begun, but the church is still closely connected to the synagogue. Jesus says they will be "handed over to local councils" and "flogged in the synagogues" (Mt 10:17).

Together these points suggest that Matthew has in mind a context in the first century, when the church is urgently proclaiming the gospel in Israel and experiencing significant persecution. Why was this task to reach Israel so urgent? The most obvious answer is the coming destruction of Jerusalem, which will serve as judgment against the nation for rejecting their Messiah. The coming of the Son of Man here most likely refers to his coming in judgment at the destruction of Jerusalem in A.D. 70, the event that confirmed his vindication at the right hand of God (Dan 7:13-14; Mk 14:62//Mt 26:64//Lk 22:69).

"Some who are standing here will not taste death." A second difficult saying appears after Jesus' teaching about the cost of discipleship in Mark 8:34-38 (//Mt 16:24-27//Lk 9:23-27). Jesus warns about the consequences of faithlessness: "If anyone is ashamed of me and my words in this adulterous and sinful generation, the Son of Man will be ashamed of them when he comes in his Father's glory with the holy angels." He then adds, "Truly I tell you, some who are standing here will not taste death before they see that the kingdom of God has come with power" (Mk 9:1). Luke has a similar saying but omits "with power" (Lk 9:27). In Matthew, Jesus speaks of "the Son of Man coming in his kingdom" (Mt 16:28) instead of "the kingdom of God" coming "with power." Jesus seems to be saying that some of his twelve disciples will be alive when the Son of Man returns and the kingdom is established.

A solution here is difficult. The passage could refer to any of the events in which the kingdom is manifested: Jesus' resurrection, his exaltation, Jerusalem's destruction or the second coming. The resurrection or exaltation would seem to be a stretch, since it is unlikely Jesus expected any of his disciples (except Judas) to die in the short time before his death and resurrection. Jesus' disciples could perhaps interpret him to be referring to casualties in a messianic war against Rome. But since these are Jesus' words (who was not envisioning such a war), this interpretation seems unlikely. Again, the destruction of Jerusalem in A.D. 70 appears to be the most likely interpretation. It will occur in forty years, a period during which some but not all of the disciples would likely die. A few would live to see the decisive judgment against Jerusalem and the temple, confirming that the new age of salvation had arrived with the life, death and resurrection of Jesus Christ.

Another common interpretation, however, is that the statement refers to the transfiguration (Mk 9:2-13//Mt 17:1-8//Lk 9:28-36), which immediately follows and serves as a preview of Jesus' glory at his exaltation and second coming. This makes good sense, since the two passages are closely connected with a time reference ("After six days"; Mk 9:2//Mt 17:1; cf. Lk 9:28). In this interpretation, three of the disciples, Peter, James and John ("some who are standing here"), will shortly experience the glory of the kingdom when the Son of Man is revealed at his transfiguration.

If we are talking about such a short time, however, it seems odd to say that some of these disciples will not die. We would not expect *any* of them to die in six days! A possible solution is that the phrase "will not taste death" is meant to contrast the three disciples who will see the glory of the kingdom *in this life* (i.e., at the transfiguration) with the rest, who will not experience it until the final resurrection.[10] A paraphrase of the passage would be something like, "A few of you will actually experience the glory of the kingdom *in this life*; indeed, you will see it in a few days."

"This generation will certainly not pass away." A third difficult passage occurs during Jesus' teaching on the Mount of Olives, his so-called Olivet Discourse (Mk 13:1-37//Mt 24:1-51//Lk 21:5-36). The disciples begin by commenting on the great beauty of the temple. Jesus responds by predicting its coming destruction, and they ask him when this will happen and what signs will accompany it. In the discourse that follows, Jesus describes the intense persecution that they will experience as they preach the gospel to all nations. He then speaks of the coming of the Son of Man:

> But in those days, following that distress,
>
> > "the sun will be darkened,
> >> and the moon will not give its light;
> > the stars will fall from the sky,
> >> and the heavenly bodies will be shaken."
>
> At that time people will see the Son of Man coming in clouds with great power and glory. And he will send his angels and gather his elect from the four winds, from the ends of the earth to the ends of the heavens. (Mk 13:24-27)

A few verses later, Jesus says, "Truly I tell you, this generation will certainly not pass away until all these things have happened" (Mk 13:30//Mt 24:34//Lk 21:32). Again, on the surface Jesus seems to identify the return of the Son of Man and the coming of the kingdom with the present generation of believers.

The Olivet Discourse is notoriously difficult to interpret, not only because it appears in three different forms (in Matthew, Mark and Luke) but also because it links the destruction of Jerusalem so closely with the coming of the Son of Man. Some commentators consider the whole discourse to be about the destruction of Jerusalem in A.D. 70. Others consider the whole thing to be about the events leading up to the second coming of Christ and the end of the age. Most see some intermingling of the two, with the former serving as a preview of the latter.

I will briefly summarize my perspective.[11] First, the destruction of Jerusalem *is* closely connected to the second coming, just as both are linked to Jesus' death, resurrection and exaltation. As we have seen, all of these events represent the outworking of God's final salvation and so may be considered eschatological. It is certainly possible that the coming of the Son of Man (Mk 13:26) refers to his coming in judgment at the destruction of Jerusalem.

It seems more likely, however, that the coming of the Son of Man in Mark 13:26 refers to the second coming, an event distinct from the destruction of Jerusalem. Apocalyptic signs accompany this event (Mk 13:24-25) and the Son of Man sends his angels to gather believers from all over the world (Mk 13:26-27), which seems to refer to the final judgment at the end of time. Here is how I would outline the discourse in Mark:

1. Events leading up to the destruction of Jerusalem (Mk 13:5-23)

2. Events related to the return of the Son of Man (Mk 13:24-27)

3. Two parables related, respectively, to each these events
   a. Parable of the fig tree related to the destruction of Jerusalem (Mk 13:28-31)
   b. Parable for watchfulness related to the second coming (Mk 13:32-37)

Verses 5-23 concern the events leading up to destruction of Jerusalem in A.D. 70. Verses 24-27 then describe the return of the Son of Man at the end of the age. This is followed by two explanatory parables, each relating to the timing of one of these events. The parable of the fig tree (vv. 28-31) concerns the destruction of Jerusalem and asserts that it will be preceded by confirming signs (vv. 28-29) and will occur within the generation of the disciples (v. 30).

The parable of the household owner (vv. 32-37), by contrast, asserts the *unknown time* of the Son of Man's return and the need for constant vigilance.

The benefit of this outline is that it helps to explain Jesus' apparently contradictory statements. In relation to the parable of the fig tree, Jesus says they will know when these events are about to take place: "Even so, when you see these things happening, you know that it is near, right at the door" (v. 29). And it will be within one generation: "Truly I tell you, this generation will certainly not pass away until all these things have happened" (v. 30). This is surely a reference to the coming destruction of Jerusalem, which will happen within one generation and will be preceded by signs to be observed. Yet a few sentences later, Jesus says, "But about that day or hour no one knows, not even the angels in heaven, nor the Son, but only the Father" (v. 32) and, "Be alert! You do not know when that time will come" (v. 33). Here he must be speaking about the second coming, which is unknown to everyone except the Father.

In summary, "this generation" in Mark 13:30 (//Mt 24:34//Lk 21:32) most likely refers to the generation of Jesus and his disciples, some of whom will live to see the destruction of Jerusalem. While these cataclysmic events certainly represent one "coming" of the Son of Man in judgment, they preview and point forward to the final judgment at the second coming of Christ and the end of the age.

"You will see the Son of Man . . . coming on the clouds." A final difficult passage occurs at Jesus' trial before the Jewish high council. When questioned by the high priest whether he is the Messiah, Jesus replies: "I am. . . . And you will see the Son of Man sitting at the right hand of the Mighty One and coming on the clouds of heaven" (Mk 14:62//Mt 26:64). In Luke's version, Jesus refers only to Jesus' exaltation: "From now on, the Son of Man will be seated at the right hand of the mighty God" (Lk 22:69).

Jesus predicts that, despite the high priest's authority over him at this time, Jesus will be vindicated by God and will judge the high priest. "Sitting at the right hand of the Mighty One" alludes to Psalm 110:1-2, a passage frequently used in the New Testament to refer to Jesus' vindication.[12] As we have seen, "coming on the clouds of heaven" alludes to Daniel 7:13-14 and could refer to the (1) exaltation, (2) destruction of Jerusalem, or (3) second coming. Any of these are possible here. Jesus' immediate vindication will come when he is exalted to the right hand of God after his resurrection. A symbolic vindication will come with the temple's destruction. An ultimate vindication will occur at the second coming.

But in what sense will the high priest and the rest of the Sanhedrin "see" Jesus in his vindication? (The "you" in Greek is plural.) A literal seeing is unlikely. If this refers to the exaltation, how could they see Jesus' heavenly enthronement at the right hand of God? If this refers to the destruction of Jerusalem, the high priest and most of the Sanhedrin would be dead by A.D. 70. The "see" here is almost certainly general and representative. The Sanhedrin, together with everyone in the world, will one day experience Jesus' vindication. Revelation 1:7 brings together Daniel 7:13 and Zechariah 12:10 to make this point:

> "Look, he is coming with the clouds,"
>> and "every eye will see him,
> even those who pierced him";
>> and all peoples on earth "will mourn because of him."

Similarly, Philippians 2:10-11 affirms that

> at the name of Jesus every knee should bow,
>> in heaven and on earth and under the earth,
> and every tongue acknowledge that Jesus Christ is Lord,
>> to the glory of God the Father.

All of creation will one day acknowledge the vindication and glory of the Son of Man.

CONCLUSION

We now live almost two thousand years since Jesus made his claim that the kingdom of God was "at hand." Did Jesus' prophecies fail? This is not a new question. Already in the first century some people were mocking Christians for false hope. The author of 2 Peter responds to scoffers who say, "Where is this 'coming' he promised?" (2 Pet 3:4). Peter's answer is twofold. First, God's timing is not our timing. To him, "a day is like a thousand years, and a thousand years are like a day" (2 Pet 3:8).[13] Second, the delay in God's judgment is motivated by his patience. He desires all people to repent and turn to him (2 Pet 3:9).

In this chapter I have sought to place Jesus' prophecies in the larger context of his ministry. Jesus came on the scene announcing the arrival of God's kingdom. Although Jesus' contemporaries hoped that the Messiah would come as a conquering king, destroying the Roman legions and establishing God's kingdom in Jerusalem, Jesus had much grander ambitions. He interpreted his mission with reference to Isaiah's prophecies of the final restoration of creation. His healings were evidence that he came to defeat the powers of disease and death. His exorcisms confirmed that he was invading Satan's realm and taking back those held in bondage to the forces of evil.

Yet Jesus described the means of salvation in a surprising way. As he headed for Jerusalem, he announced his intention to suffer and die there. At his Last Supper he explained the significance of his death. His body and blood given as a sacrifice would accomplish a new Passover and a new exodus. His death would bring forgiveness of sins and establish a new covenant relationship with God.

These are remarkable claims. But are they true? If not, then Jesus was one more tragic story in Israel's history. If they are true, he is the victorious King and Savior of the world. The significance of world history is riding on the question. According to the Gospels,

Jesus claimed that after his death God would vindicate him by raising him from the dead.

The truth or falsity of Christianity depends on what happened after Jesus' death. In our last chapter we will turn to that question.

Decaying Corpse
or Resurrected Lord?

All the Eggs in
One Easter Basket

THE RESURRECTION OF JESUS IS, of course, the most controversial and debated event in Jesus' life (and perhaps human
history).[1] If Jesus indeed rose from the dead, then the claims he made
about himself were vindicated. If he did not rise, then whatever claims
he made were the words of a deluded prophet or a madman. The
apostle Paul speaks of this all-or-nothing aspect of the resurrection:

> If Christ has not been raised, our preaching is useless and so
> is your faith. More than that, we are then found to be false
> witnesses about God, for we have testified about God that he
> raised Christ from the dead. . . . And if Christ has not been
> raised, your faith is futile; you are still in your sins. . . . If only
> for this life we have hope in Christ, we are of all people most
> to be pitied. (1 Cor 15:14-15, 17, 19)

Paul says that the gospel message rises or falls on the reality of the
resurrection. Christianity has all of its eggs in one basket—and it is
an Easter basket.

A Curious Resurrection Announcement

A book can hardly talk about the puzzling and enigmatic words and actions of Jesus without discussing the resurrection, the most puzzling and enigmatic of them all. Indeed, the earliest account of the resurrection in the Gospels—the one recorded in Mark—is a peculiar episode. Mark 16:1-8 reads,

> When the Sabbath was over, Mary Magdalene, Mary the mother of James, and Salome bought spices so that they might go to anoint Jesus' body. Very early on the first day of the week, just after sunrise, they were on their way to the tomb and they asked each other, "Who will roll the stone away from the entrance of the tomb?"
>
> But when they looked up, they saw that the stone, which was very large, had been rolled away. As they entered the tomb, they saw a young man dressed in a white robe sitting on the right side, and they were alarmed.
>
> "Don't be alarmed," he said. "You are looking for Jesus the Nazarene, who was crucified. He has risen! He is not here. See the place where they laid him. But go, tell his disciples and Peter, 'He is going ahead of you into Galilee. There you will see him, just as he told you.'"
>
> Trembling and bewildered, the women went out and fled from the tomb. They said nothing to anyone, because they were afraid. (Mk 16:1-8)

At this point our earliest manuscripts of Mark end. There are no resurrection appearances and no report given to the (male) disciples. The women are terrified and remain silent. So what happened? Did they ever see the resurrected Jesus? Did they get over their fear and report to the disciples what they had seen? Did the other disciples see Jesus alive? Mark does not say.

To be fair, we have to acknowledge that the author of Mark's

Gospel believed the resurrection took place. Some have claimed that there is no resurrection in Mark, but this is not true. Jesus, a completely reliable character whose predictions always come true, repeatedly predicts his death *and resurrection* (Mk 8:31; 9:9, 31; 10:33-34; 14:28; 16:7). The angel also announces it (Mk 16:6). (If you can't trust an angel, who can you trust?) Furthermore, by the time Mark wrote (likely in the late A.D. 60s), the church had been proclaiming the resurrection for decades. What is curiously missing in Mark's story is not the resurrection but resurrection appearances to the disciples.

There is a longer ending to Mark's Gospel that appears in many later manuscripts, which recounts resurrection appearances (i.e., Mk 16:9-20); but almost all scholars agree that this ending was added by a later copyist to smooth over Mark's awkward ending. Its style and content are different from Mark's own style and themes, and it doesn't appear in our earliest and best manuscripts.[2] So how do we explain Mark's abrupt ending? Some scholars think that the last page of Mark's Gospel was lost. Others believe that Mark intentionally ended his Gospel on this mysterious note, perhaps to call his readers to respond to the resurrection announcement with faith, just like the women are called to do.

In any case, the other Gospels fill in the blanks, recounting a series of resurrection appearances. Matthew describes the discovery of the empty tomb and the announcement of the resurrection by an angel (Mt 28:1-7), followed by resurrection appearances to the women (Mt 28:8-10) and later appearances to the eleven disciples in Galilee (Mt 28:16-20). Luke records the discovery of the empty tomb by the women and the announcement of the resurrection by two angels (Lk 24:1-12). This is followed by appearances to two of Jesus' disciples on the road to Emmaus near Jerusalem (Lk 24:13-35) and then an appearance to the eleven disciples in Jerusalem (Lk 24:36-49). This is followed by Jesus' ascension (Lk

24:50-53), an event that takes place forty days after the resurrection in Luke's second volume (Acts 1:1-11). In John, Mary Magdalene (presumably alone) discovers the empty tomb and reports it to Peter and the Beloved Disciple (John?), who investigate (Jn 20:1-10). Jesus then appears to Mary Magdalene (Jn 20:11-18) and then to the disciples in Jerusalem, first without Thomas (Jn 20:24-25) and then a week later with Thomas present (Jn 20:26-29). Jesus then appears one last time later at the Sea of Galilee, where he produces a miraculous catch of fish (Jn 21:1-23).

Many questions are raised by these accounts: Did a group of women (Mk 16:1) or Mary Magdalene alone (Jn 20:1) discover the empty tomb? Who announced the resurrection, a young man (Mk 16:5), an angel (Mt 28:2) or two "men" in gleaming clothes (Lk 24:4)? Did the women see Jesus alive at this time (Mt 28:9), or did they go away confused and bewildered (Mk 16:8)? Did Mary see Jesus alone (Jn 20:11-13) or with the other women (Mt 28:9)? Did the disciples disbelieve the report of the women (Lk 24:11), or did Peter and the Beloved Disciple run to the tomb to investigate, and believe (Jn 20:3-10)? Did the Eleven first see Jesus in Galilee (Mt 26:32; 28:10, 16-20; Mk 14:28; 16:7) or in Jerusalem (Lk 24; Jn 20)? Did Jesus' ascension to heaven take place just after the resurrection (Lk 24:50-51) or forty days later (Acts 1:3-11)?

It is certainly possible to harmonize these events and work out a plausible chronology.[3] But it is not easy. Bart Ehrman challenges such reconstructions:

> Read the accounts for yourself. . . . They in fact differ at almost every point. And it isn't just a matter of one account adding some detail not found in another, or giving a slightly different spin on the story. Sometimes the differences seem nearly impossible to reconcile.[4]

Ehrman makes no such attempt at harmonization. This is because he rejects the historicity of the resurrection primarily for philosophical reasons. Though he claims not to be working from an assumption of antisupernaturalism (since anything is possible), he considers miracles to be *virtually impossible*. He writes,

> Historians more or less rank past events on the basis of the relative probability that they occurred. . . .
>
> [B]ut miracles, by their very nature, are always the least probable explanation for what happened. This is true whether you are a believer or not. . . .
>
> The resurrection is not least likely because of any anti-Christian bias. It is the least likely because people do not come back to life, never to die again.[5]

WORLDVIEW CONSIDERATIONS

Ehrman's assertions about miracles echo those of eighteenth-century Scottish philosopher David Hume, who claimed that in light of the inviolable laws of nature, a miracle to be true would have to achieve an impossibly high standard of evidence.[6]

But, as many have pointed out, this argument is circular. It begins with the *presupposition* that miracles are the least likely explanation for any event and so concludes that no miracle is demonstrable. Yet as Craig Keener has pointed out in his recent volume on miracles, Hume is working in a deductive circle: "He argues based on 'experience,' that miracles do not happen, yet dismisses credible eyewitness testimony for miracles (i.e., *others'* experience) on his assumption that miracles do not happen."[7]

In response Keener marshals a massive body of evidence throughout history and from diverse cultures around the world of credible eyewitness accounts of miracles. Hundreds of millions of people claim to have experienced miracles, essentially nullifying Hume's claims that they only occur among primitive, naive and ignorant people. It is time, Keener argues, to reassess these anti-supernatural presuppositions.[8]

This is not to say we should accept an uncritical stance toward the supernatural or assume that every report of the miraculous is equally valid. There are certainly gullible people around, and deceit and fraud do take place. But which is more objective, to assume ahead of time that a miracle cannot happen or to adopt an open but cautious approach? A miracle should be acknowledged if those who report it demonstrate a high degree of credibility and if there is sufficient eyewitness testimony to corroborate it.

What, then, can we say about Jesus' resurrection? Is there credible historical evidence for it, or are there better rationalistic explanations?

RATIONALISTIC EXPLANATIONS FOR THE RESURRECTION

Through the years various proposals have been made to explain the resurrection accounts on rationalistic grounds. Some have claimed that the women got confused and went to the wrong tomb. Others think the disciples stole the body of Jesus and faked a resurrection. Still others say Jesus never died on the cross. He swooned or went into a coma, later waking up, escaping the tomb and announcing that he was alive.

None of these particular theories hold much water. The wrong tomb theory seems ludicrous, since it would mean that everyone went to the wrong tomb, not just the women but the disciples, Jesus' enemies and even Joseph of Arimathea—who owned the tomb! It seems equally unlikely that the disciples stole the body. All the evidence indicates that they were devastated and discouraged by the rejection and crucifixion of their teacher. Nothing would be gained by pretending it was not so. We also have to wonder how these same disciples, who developed the highest ethical system in the world and placed the greatest premium on truth, in fact perpetuated a great lie. The idea that Jesus did not die on the cross is also implausible. The Romans were experts at what they did, and it is inconceivable that they would have botched the job. In any case, no one would have confused a half-dead Jesus who barely survived crucifixion with the glorious Savior who rose victorious over death. Mere survival could not have provoked Easter faith.[9]

Few scholars hold to any of these theories. Most who reject the historicity of the resurrection argue instead that resurrection faith likely arose as a result of dreams or visions that the disciples had after Jesus' death. These convinced the disciples that Jesus was in some sense spiritually alive and had been vindicated by God. Over time these ideas developed into legends of resurrection appearances. Ehrman is representative of this view when he writes: "Jesus' closest followers, and later Paul, claimed they saw him alive afterward. Does it mean he was really raised from the dead? No, it means that they, like so many thousands of other people had a real-seeming, tangible experience of a person after he died."[10] This "vision and legendary development theory" is really the only widely asserted challenge to the resurrection today.

So what is the evidence for an actual bodily resurrection? In the discussion that follows, we will *not* assume the inspiration or authority of the Bible, or the necessary reliability of the Gospel accounts. Instead, we will ask what historical facts related to the resurrection can be shown to be true *beyond reasonable doubt* when placed under critical scrutiny.

EVIDENCE RELATED TO THE RESURRECTION

The first piece of nearly indisputable evidence is that *Jesus died by crucifixion around A.D. 30*. Through the years there have been occasional claims by skeptics that Jesus never existed. But no credible historian believes this. Nor can it be denied that Jesus was crucified under the jurisdiction of the Roman prefect Pontius Pilate around

A.D. 30–33. We have not only Christian but also Jewish (Josephus), and Roman (Tacitus) sources identifying Pilate as responsible for Jesus' execution.[11] Jesus' death by crucifixion is the most indisputable fact about his life.

Second, we can say with near certainty that after Jesus' death *his body was buried in the tomb of a man named Joseph of Arimathea.* Some scholars have asserted that Jesus, like many other crucified victims, was denied a burial and that his body was either eaten as carrion or thrown into a common grave.[12] This claim is intended to negate accounts of the empty tomb. If there were no tomb, it could not have been discovered empty three days later.

But the burial account has a very high probability of authenticity. It is attested in multiple sources, including the Synoptic Gospels (Mk 15:43-47; Mt 27:57-61; Lk 23:50-54), John (Jn 19:38-42), Acts (Acts 2:31; 13:36-38) and by Paul (1 Cor 15:3-4). Paul, writing about A.D. 55, claims to have received this tradition from Christians before him. Since Paul became a follower of Jesus around A.D. 35, we are talking about very early tradition.

It also seems unlikely that the church would have created a story with so specific a name as "Joseph of Arimathea" attached to it. Where did the name come from? Joseph's hometown of Arimathea does not seem to have any symbolic significance. Such a creation would be especially odd since Joseph is identified as a member of the Sanhedrin, the Jewish high council (Mk 15:43//Lk 23:50). Would the church have created a story in which a member of the judicial body that condemned Jesus in fact gave him a noble burial? Matthew omits any mention of Joseph's association with the Sanhedrin (Mt 27:57), perhaps out of embarrassment.

A third practically indisputable fact is that *on the third day after Jesus' burial, his tomb was discovered empty.* All four Gospels testify to this (Mt 28:1-7; Mk 16:1-8; Lk 24:1-8; Jn 20:1-18). Paul also testifies that the resurrection occurred on the third day (1 Cor 15:4). Though the accounts of the tomb's discovery differ somewhat in detail, all agree that it was *women* who discovered the empty tomb. This is remarkable, since women were not considered reliable witnesses in first-century Judaism. The church would never have invented stories in which women discovered the empty tomb.

There are other incidental details that point to an empty tomb. Matthew reports an accusation from the church's Jewish opponents that the disciples stole the body of Jesus (Mt 28:11-15). The church is unlikely to have created such an accusation unless it was actually being made. And the claim to a stolen body of course assumes that the body is missing.

Finally, we know that the followers of Jesus were preaching about the resurrection in Jerusalem shortly after Jesus' death. If the body were still in the tomb, Jesus' opponents would easily have refuted this claim by producing the body.

A fourth practically indisputable fact is that *the disciples of Jesus claimed to have seen him alive shortly after his death.* From its earliest days the preaching about the resurrection was central to the message of the early church. The earliest written account of resurrection appearances comes from Paul, who writes,

> For what I received I passed on to you as of first importance: that Christ died for our sins according to the Scriptures, that he was buried, that he was raised on the third day according to the Scriptures, and that he appeared to Cephas [Peter], and then to the Twelve. After that, he appeared to more than five hundred of the brothers and sisters at the same time, most of whom are still living, though some have fallen asleep. Then he appeared to James, then to all the apostles, and last of all he appeared to me also, as to one abnormally born. (1 Cor 15:3-8)

Many incidental references confirm the reality of resurrection appearances. The appearance to Peter (Cephas), for example, is independently attested by Paul and in Luke 24:34. The appearance to the Eleven is also independently confirmed in multiple sources: Paul, the Synoptic Gospels and John. The appearance to James, the half brother of Jesus, is recorded only in 1 Corinthians 15:5, but makes historical sense. Though Jesus' brothers did not believe in him during his ministry (Mk 3:21; Jn 7:5), they became leaders in the church shortly after his resurrection (Acts 1:14; 12:17; 1 Cor 9:5; Gal 1:19). A resurrection appearance makes sense of this change of heart.

The resurrection appearances to female disciples also argue strongly for the authenticity of these accounts. As noted earlier, women were not considered reliable witnesses in Judaism, so the church would never have invented stories where women were the first witnesses of the resurrection.

Even many scholars who are agnostic or unbelieving acknowledge that the disciples *truly believed* that they had seen Jesus alive. David Friedrich Strauss, the eighteenth-century skeptic who popularized the view that the entire Gospel miracle tradition is myth, affirmed that it was virtually certain "that the Apostles themselves had the conviction that they had seen the risen Jesus."[13] Respected German New Testament scholar Gerd Lüdemann, who has repeatedly engaged in debates seeking to refute the resurrection, writes, "It may be taken as historically certain that Peter and the disciples had experiences after Jesus' death in which Jesus appeared to them as the risen Christ."[14] Paula Fredriksen, author of the critically acclaimed *From Jesus to Christ*, writes, "We can draw securely from this evidence only the baldest conclusion: that despite the absolute certainty of Jesus' death, his immediate followers with equal certainty perceived—and then proclaimed—that Jesus lived again."[15] E. P. Sanders, who is agnostic about the resurrection, writes, "That Jesus' followers (and later Paul) had resurrection experiences is, in my judgment, a fact."[16] None of these scholars expresses belief in the resurrection, but all are convinced that the disciples had some kind of experiences of the resurrected Lord.

But could these appearances have been merely visionary experiences or hopeful dreams? Some have pointed out that Paul's experience of the risen Christ, which he interprets as a resurrection appearance in 1 Corinthians 15:8, was itself visionary. But Paul's point here is to show that he too had a commission from the resurrected Christ, not to assert that his experience was the same as the other apostles. In fact, he refers to the appearance to him as unique—"as to one abnormally born" (1 Cor 15:8).

While it is certainly possible that the early Christians had visions or dreams about Jesus, phenomena like this tend to have a different qualitative nature than actual human encounters.[17] The resurrection appearances in the Gospels describe Jesus talking, eating and even touching the disciples (Lk 24:39-43; Jn 20:24-28). Visions and dreams also tend to be personal and subjective rather than social and communal. Yet Paul says that Jesus appeared to five hundred people at one time (1 Cor 15:6).

Nor does a merely spiritual or visionary resurrection fit the worldview of the disciples. Those groups in Judaism that believed in a future resurrection—like the Pharisees and the Essenes—expected it to be a bodily resurrection that took place at the end of time as part of the final judgment. This is Paul's primary point in 1 Corinthians 15:35-54. Against the Greek dualistic view of a merely spiritual afterlife, he argues that our resurrection, like Christ's, will be a *bodily one*. Paul would not have said that Jesus was "the first-fruits of those who have fallen asleep" (1 Cor 15:20) or "the beginning and the firstborn from among the dead" (Col 1:18) if for him the resurrection was merely a vision of Jesus' spirit after his death.

As N. T. Wright points out, neither the empty tomb nor resurrection appearances alone would by necessity have created early Christian belief. The discovery of an empty tomb alone would have been viewed as a puzzle and a tragedy. Grave robbery was common, and the body of Jesus could have been moved or stolen. Resurrection appearances alone could be viewed as visionary experiences or hopeful dreams. But the two combined, together with the disciples' conviction that Jesus was the Messiah whose role was to establish the kingdom, convinced them that Jesus had risen bodily from the dead.[18] This is the faith that they proclaimed.

This brings us to a fifth practically indisputable fact, which is *the changed lives of the disciples.* We have already noted two individuals whose radical change of heart following the resurrection is historically verifiable. The apostle Paul, by his own testimony, was a persecutor of the church until he had a personal encounter with the resurrected Jesus (1 Cor 9:1; 15:8; Gal 1:13-16; Phil 3:6; cf. Acts 9, 22, 26). This is a primary source testimony. Jesus' half brother James also did not believe in him during Jesus' public ministry (Mk 3:21; Jn 7:5). But he became a leader in the early church after the resurrection (Acts 1:14; 12:17; 15:13; 21:18; 1 Cor 9:5; Gal 1:19). What would convince any of us that our own brother was the Son of God and Savior of the world? A resurrection appearance would be a pretty good start (1 Cor 15:7).

Finally, we have to consider the level of conviction exhibited by the apostles. Many suffered and died for their faith. People are often willing to die for something that they believe to be true but turns out to be false (consider the tragedies of the People's Temple in Jonestown and the Branch Davidians in Waco). But they seldom sacrifice themselves for something they *know* to be untrue.[19] What convinced Jesus' disciples that the message of an executed Jewish prophet was worth dying for? Their own answer is that they had seen him alive.

CONCLUSION: A LIVING FAITH

Together these five practically indisputable facts would seem to produce a formidable case for the resurrection. At least they do for me. Of course not everyone will see it this way. The conclusion people draw will depend to a great extent on their background, worldview and prior commitment to faith or skepticism.

So in conclusion I'd like to return to where we began in this chapter, with that mysterious account of the resurrection in Mark's Gospel. The women are left with two key pieces of evidence, the empty tomb and the announcement that Jesus is alive. Their initial response is confusion and fear. But the story ends with this implicit question: How will they ultimately respond, with faith or with fear? In many ways, we are in the same boat. We are confronted with the same evidence and must respond with either faith or with skepticism.

Yet when we look ahead at the story of the early church, we see it was not just the evidence of the resurrection that sustained Jesus' followers. It was their continuing experience of him as their living Lord. It was his presence experienced in the worship of the community and through their celebration of the Lord's Supper. It was the empowering presence of his Spirit that they had received on the day of Pentecost and experienced daily. It was his continuing voice communicated through prayer and in the words of Christian teachers and prophets. It was the experiential evidence of transformed lives.

For these believers Jesus was not the Messiah who was once present but had now gone away. He was their living and present Lord, now guiding his church to proclaim his lordship and announce his kingdom. Knowing *about* Jesus is one thing; knowing him is something else.

From a historical perspective, Jesus remains in many ways a fascinating, mysterious and enigmatic figure. We can certainly build a credible case for who he was and what he hoped to accomplish. But this will only take us so far. Coming to know Jesus is more than just learning the events of his life. It is about experiencing his daily presence. For those who have walked with him through life's peaks and valleys and who experience his daily presence in their lives, Jesus is more than a figure of history. He is Savior and Lord, the source of meaning and hope.

If this book accomplishes anything, I hope it has piqued your interest in getting to know Jesus more, both through his words and actions in the Gospels and through a personal encounter with the living Lord.

Discussion Questions

Chapter 1: Everybody Likes Jesus

1. How would you answer the question, Who was Jesus Christ?

2. How would different people you know answer this question?

3. What is your favorite saying from or story about Jesus? Why?

4. What in your view is the most difficult or disturbing saying or action of Jesus?

5. What do you think of Bertrand Russell's claim that Jesus was unethical because he cursed a fig tree, caused the death of thousands of pigs and believed that many people would go to hell?

Chapter 2: Revolutionary or Pacifist?

1. According to the author, why was Palestine ripe for revolution in Jesus' day?

2. Summarize some of the key evidence the author offers that Jesus was a revolutionary.

3. What do you think Jesus meant when he said, "The kingdom of God has come near"?

4. In what sense does the coming of the kingdom mean the restoration of a fallen creation?

5. How does Jesus define his role as the Messiah in Luke 7:18-23// Matthew 11:2-6?

6. What do Jesus' miracles signify? (What foes does he claim to be defeating through his miracles?)

7. So, where do you come down—was Jesus a revolutionary, a pacifist or something else? Explain.

CHAPTER 3: ANGRY OR LOVING?

1. According to the author, why did the religious leaders in Israel have problems with Jesus?

2. What did Jesus say about the religious leaders? How did he insult them?

3. What does the chapter say about who the Pharisees and the Sadducees were?

4. In what ways was Jesus a threat to the Pharisees' and the Sadducees' authority?

5. What provocative actions did Jesus do during his last Passover visit to Jerusalem?

6. Do you think Jesus' anger was justified on these occasions? Why or why not?

CHAPTER 4: ENVIRONMENTALIST OR EARTH SCORCHER?

1. Why did Jesus allow the demons to get their way and enter the pigs?

2. Was this an act of irresponsibility on Jesus' part? Why or why not?

3. What do we learn about demons from this episode?

4. What do we learn about Jesus' mission?

5. Why did Jesus curse the fig tree?

6. Do you think this was a childish and capricious act? Why or why not?

7. How does the author say the fig tree incident related to Jesus' clearing of the temple courts?

8. What do these episodes teach us about Jesus' identity as the "new temple" of God?

CHAPTER 5: LEGALIST OR GRACE FILLED?

1. How would you define *legalism*?

2. Would you say Jesus was a legalist? Why or why not?

3. What is the evidence in Jesus' teaching (especially the parables) that people are saved by receiving God's free gift of salvation, not by earning it through works?

4. How does the story of the rich young ruler illustrate that salvation comes through faith in God alone, apart from our good works?

5. How would you explain Jesus' apparent call for self-mutilation (cut off your hand or gouge out your eye)? Did he expect his followers to actually do this?

6. In what ways can our righteousness surpass that of the Pharisees and teachers of the law?

7. What role does the Holy Spirit play in enabling believers to live righteous lives?

8. So, what is your opinion? Was Jesus a legalist or not? Explain.

CHAPTER 6: HELLFIRE PREACHER OR GENTLE SHEPHERD?

1. What do you think about churches that open "Hell Houses" as a motivation for evangelism?

2. What are some of the different views of hell held by Christians? Which do you think is most likely and why?

3. What did Jesus teach about hell?

4. The chapter argues that the doctrine of hell (or divine punishment) is essential to the goodness and justice of God. Do you agree? Why or why not?

CHAPTER 7: ANTIFAMILY OR FAMILY FRIENDLY?

1. What is the evidence that Jesus was profamily?

2. What is the evidence that Jesus considered spiritual family relationships to supersede physical ones?

3. What did Jesus mean when he said that to be his disciple one must "hate" their own family members (Lk 14:26)?

4. In the first-century Greco-Roman world, what challenges did new believers in Jesus face in relation to their own family and their society's values?

5. In what ways do Christians around the world today face these same struggles?

6. What did Jesus promise for those willing to leave behind their family and possessions for the kingdom of God?

7. How should Jesus' teaching about family impact us today?

CHAPTER 8: RACIST OR INCLUSIVIST?

1. What are some examples of racism or ethnocentricity in our world today?

2. What examples of experiencing racism do you have from your own life or that of someone you know?

3. What is some of the evidence for Jesus' ethnocentricity (his favoritism for the Jews)?

4. What did Jesus mean when he called the Syrophoenician woman a "dog" (Mt 15:26//Mk 7:27)?

5. Why did Jesus first send his disciples to preach only to the people of Israel?

6. What is the evidence that Jesus intended the good news of salvation to be for all people everywhere?

7. How does Jesus' sermon at Nazareth illustrate his vision for salvation for all people (Lk 4:14-30)?

8. What other passages in the Gospels point to the inclusive nature of salvation (that it is intended for all people everywhere)?

9. How should Christians respond today to racism and ethnocentricity?

CHAPTER 9: SEXIST OR EGALITARIAN?

1. How were women generally viewed in the Judaism of Jesus' day? What was their social status?

2. What is the evidence that Jesus affirmed the value and dignity of women?

3. What is the evidence that Jesus shared the more negative views of his countrymen?

4. Some conservative Christians view themselves as *complementarians* and some as *egalitarians*. What do these two terms mean?

5. How would each group explain Jesus' choice of twelve male apostles?

6. Which perspective do you think is more true to Jesus' vision and why?

CHAPTER 10: WAS JESUS ANTI-SEMITIC?

1. What are some ways anti-Semitism has manifested itself in the history of the church?

2. Why is it anachronistic to ask the question, Was Jesus anti-Jewish?

3. Why did Jesus challenge and denounce the religious leaders of his day?

4. How do we explain the strong language related to "the Jews" in John's Gospel?

5. Did the early followers of Jesus intend to start a new religion? Explain.

6. What were the early Christians trying to do?

7. How should Christians today relate to people of the Jewish faith?

CHAPTER 11: FAILED PROPHET OR VICTORIOUS KING?

1. What have been some of the negative or destructive consequences of end-of-the-world predictions?

2. What is the evidence that Jesus himself predicted the soon end of the world?

3. According to Albert Schweitzer and Bart Ehrman (and others), Jesus was a *failed* apocalyptic prophet. What does this mean?

4. What did Jesus mean by "kingdom of God"?

5. This chapter argues that the coming of the kingdom of God is a complex and multiphase event. What are the various events that signal the arrival of the kingdom?

6. How do Jesus' words instituting the Lord's Supper reveal the meaning of his impending death?

7. In what sense is Jesus' resurrection related to the coming of the kingdom of God and God's final judgment?

8. How is the pouring out of the Spirit on the day of Pentecost

related to the coming of the kingdom and the glorification of the Son of Man (Dan 7:13-14)?

9. In light of this chapter, how would you summarize what you believe about the coming kingdom of God?

CHAPTER 12: DECAYING CORPSE OR RESURRECTED LORD?

1. Why does the apostle Paul consider the resurrection of Jesus to be such a critically important historical event?

2. What makes Mark's narrative about the resurrection so puzzling (Mark 16:1-8)?

3. David Hume (among others) objected to miracles because they violated laws of nature. Do you find this convincing? Why or why not?

4. What nonsupernatural explanations have been given for the resurrection accounts?

5. What are the five pieces of "nearly indisputable" evidence related to the resurrection presented in this chapter?

6. What are problems or difficulties with any of these?

7. As you look back over the book, what words or actions of Jesus do you still find troubling and why?

8. How has your appreciation and understanding of Jesus grown in the course of reading the book?

Notes

Chapter 1: Everybody Likes Jesus

[1]"Jesus Is Just Alright," written by Arthur Reid Reynolds, 1966, was made a hit in the United States when it was included on the Doobie Brothers' 1972 album *Toulouse Street*.

[2]Lk 14:26; Mt 18:8-9//Mk 9:43-48; Mt 5:29-30; 19:12; Jn 6:53-56. The symbol // refers to a parallel passage, usually among the Synoptic Gospels (Matthew, Mark, Luke).

[3]Russell delivered this lecture on March 6, 1927, to the National Secular Society, South London Branch, at Battersea Town Hall. It was published in pamphlet form and then republished in Russell's book, *Why I Am Not a Christian and Other Essays* (New York: Touchstone, 1957). It is available online at users.drew.edu/~jlenz/whynot.html. In reality, Russell claims to doubt Jesus even existed, but his point is that the Jesus of the Gospels (and so of Christianity) had serious moral defects.

[4]This quote is frequently attributed to Mark Twain (search the web and you'll see hundreds of examples), but I could not find it in any of his writings. It may be apocryphal.

Chapter 2: Revolutionary or Pacifist?

[1]Josephus, *Jewish Wars* 2.13.3 §§254-55.

[2]Ibid., 2.8.1 §118; Josephus, *Antiquities of the Jews* 18.1.6 §23; 18.1.1 §§5-7; cf. Acts 5:37.

[3]Josephus, *Antiquities of the Jews* 20.5.2 §102.

[4]Ibid., 20 §§97-98. It is debated whether the Theudas of Acts 5:36 is the same man or an earlier rebel, since Luke seems to place him much earlier in the first century (before Judas of Galilee in A.D. 4).

[5]Josephus, *Jewish Wars* 2.13.5 §§261-63; *Antiquities of the Jews* 20.8.6 §§169-72; Acts 21:38.

[6]Of course Simon could have been a religious zealot, that is, passionate about his faith, not a violent revolutionary. Or he could have been a *former* zealot, who left behind his violent past to follow the more pacifist Jesus. Further complicating the picture is the fact that while Josephus refers to the "Zealots" as a "fourth philosophy" of Judaism (in addition to the Pharisees, Sadducees and Essenes), some scholars have argued that the title itself was not actually used for a specific opposition group until the Jewish revolt of A.D. 66–74. This raises further questions, at least, about the nature of Simon's zealotry.

[7]"Psalms of Solomon: A New Translation and Introduction," in *The Old Testament Pseudepigrapha*, trans. R. B. Wright, ed. J. S. Charlesworth (Garden City, NY: Doubleday, 1985), 2:667.

[8]*Rule of the Community* (1QS) 1:9-10; cf. 1QS 2:24; 5:25; *War Scroll* (1QM) 1:1.

[9]See Robert Ellsberg, ed., *Gandhi on Christianity* (Maryknoll, NY: Orbis Books, 1991); and the sermon by Martin Luther King Jr., "Loving Your Enemies," Dexter Avenue Baptist Church, November 17, 1957, http://mlk -kpp01.stanford.edu/index.php/encyclopedia/documentsentry/doc _loving_your_enemies.

[10]Josephus, *Antiquities of the Jews* 18.5.2 §§116-19.

CHAPTER 3: ANGRY OR LOVING?

[1]For other statements of popularity see Mk 1:37; 2:2, 4, 13; 3:7-9, 20; 4:1, 36; 5:21, 24, 30-32; 6:14-15, 31-34; 7:24; 8:1-3; 9:14-15, 30; 10:1, 13; 11:18; 12:12, 37; 14:1-2 and parallels in the other Gospels.

CHAPTER 4: ENVIRONMENTALIST OR EARTH SCORCHER?

[1]See, for example, the healing of Jairus's daughter in Matthew 9:18-26, which is less than half the length of Mark's parallel in Mark 5:21-43.

[2]T. W. Manson, "The Cleansing of the Temple," *Bulletin of the John Ry- lands Library* 33 (1951): 259.

[3]Bertrand Russell, *Why I Am Not a Christian and Other Essays* (New York: Touchstone, 1957), 19.

CHAPTER 5: LEGALIST OR GRACE FILLED?

[1]Institute in Basic Life Principles was formerly called Institute in Basic Youth Conflicts. See the Institute in Basic Life Principles website (www .iblp.org) for the history of the organization and of Gothard's seminars.

[2]Alissa Wilkinson, "A Sound Foundation," *Alissa Wilkinson* blog, February 28, 2014, www.alissawilkinson.com/blog/a-sound-foundation.

[3]Ibid.

[4]Sara (Roberts) Jones, "Dear Mr. Gothard: One Student's Letter," *Recovering Grace*, January 24, 2013, www.recoveringgrace.org/2013/01/dear-mr-gothard-one-students-letter.

[5]This description of the man comes from harmonizing the Gospels. All three Synoptics call him rich, but only Luke calls him a "ruler" (Lk 18:18) and only Matthew says he was young (Mt 19:20).

[6]Rabbi Acha (c. A.D. 320) in *Leviticus Rabbah* 35.6.

[7]*Lamentations Rabbah* 1.34.

[8]R. T. France, *The Gospel of Matthew*, New International Commentary (Grand Rapids: Eerdmans, 2007), 748-49.

[9]See Deut 28:1-14; Job 1:10; 42:10; Ps 128:1-2; Prov 10:22; Is 3:10; Sirach 11:17; 31:5-10.

[10]R. H. Gundry, *Mark: A Commentary on His Apology for the Cross* (Grand Rapids: Eerdmans, 1993), 565.

CHAPTER 6: HELLFIRE PREACHER OR GENTLE SHEPHERD?

[1]Paul speaks occasionally of the punishment and destruction of the wicked in 1 Thessalonians 5:3 and 2 Thessalonians 1:6-9, but not of hell per se.

[2]See 1 Enoch 26-27; 90:26; 2 Esdras 7:36; 2 Baruch 59:5-11.

[3]A third term, *Tartarus*, appears only in 2 Peter 2:4. It can refer to a place of torment and punishment after death.

[4]See Mike Floorwalker, "10 Terrifying Unsolved Serial Murders," *Listverse*, April 17, 2013, www.listverse.com/2013/04/17/10-terrifying-unsolved-serial-murders. See also "Top 10 Unsolved Crimes," *Time*, accessed March 27, 2015, http://content.time.com/time/specials/packages/completelist/0,29569,1867198,00.html.

[5]For a recent defense of this view see the various essays in C. W. Morgan and R. A. Peterson, eds., *Hell Under Fire: Modern Scholarship Reinvents Eternal Punishment* (Grand Rapids: Zondervan, 2004).

[6]For a recent defense of this view see Sharon L. Baker, *Razing Hell: Rethinking Everything You've Been Taught About God's Wrath and Judgment* (Louisville: Westminster John Knox, 2010); cf. Rob Bell, *Love Wins: A Book About Heaven, Hell, and the Fate of Every Person Who Ever Lived* (New York: HarperOne, 2011).

[7]See also Jn 3:18; 5:29; 12:25, 48; Acts 13:46; 28:24-27; Rom 2:5-12; 6:23; 1 Cor 6:9-10; Gal 6:7-8; 2 Cor 4:3-4; Eph 5:6; Col 3:6, 25; Phil 1:28; 3:19; 1 Tim 4:16; 5:24; 6:9; Heb 3:14-19; 6:4-8; 10:26-31, 39; 2 Pet 2:3, 6, 9-10, 17, 20-22; 3:7, 16; 1 Jn 2:19; 3:10, 15; 5:16; Rev 20:11-15; 22:15.

[8]For defenses of annihilationism, see Edward William Fudge, *The Fire That Consumes: A Biblical and Historical Study of the Doctrine of Final Punishment*, 3rd ed. (Eugene, OR: Wipf & Stock, 2011); David L. Edwards and John R. W. Stott, *Evangelical Essentials: A Liberal-Evangelical Dialogue* (Downers Grove, IL: InterVarsity Press, 1988); David Hilborn, ed., *The Nature of Hell: A Report by the Evangelical Alliance Commission on Unity and Truth Among Evangelicals* (Carlisle, UK: ACUTE/Paternoster, 2000).

[9]Edwards and Stott, *Evangelical Essentials*, 316.

Chapter 7: Antifamily or Family Friendly?

[1]Ronald Enroth, *Youth, Brainwashing, and the Extremist Cults* (Grand Rapids: Zondervan, 1977), 84. Similar case studies can be found throughout Enroth's book.

[2]See James R. Lewis, *The Encyclopedia of Cults, Sects, and New Religions* (Amherst, NY: Prometheus, 1998); and his *Cults: A Reference Handbook*, Contemporary World Issues (Santa Barbara: ABC-CLIO, 2005).

[3]Eusebius, *Church History* 6.8. This story is doubted by some historians today.

[4]R. T. France, *The Gospel of Matthew*, New International Commentary on the New Testament (Grand Rapids: Eerdmans, 2007), 723-24.

[5]This story and similar ones can be found in the movie *More Than Dreams* (Worcester, PA: Vision Video, 2007). The stories are told by the participants themselves and claim independent verification.

[6]Joseph Hellerman, *When the Church Was a Family: Recapturing Jesus' Vision for Authentic Christian Community* (Nashville: B & H Publishing, 2009), 74.

[7]F. F. Bruce, *The Hard Sayings of Jesus* (Downers Grove, IL: IVP Academic, 1983), 120.

Chapter 8: Racist or Inclusivist?

[1]Mary Beard, "Racism in Greece and Rome," in *The Times Literary Supplement*, January 22, 2007, http://timesonline.typepad.com/dons_life/2007/01/racism_in_greec.html.

[2]In Luke's version, Jewish elders from Capernaum approach Jesus with the man's request. In Matthew the centurion himself makes the request. Matthew is likely abbreviating the account: the request came from the centurion through Jewish intermediaries.

CHAPTER 9: SEXIST OR EGALITARIAN?

[1]Josephus, *Against Apion* 2.25 §201.

[2]Josephus, *Antiquities of the Jews* 4.8.15 §219.

[3]Philo, *Embassy to Gaius* 40 (319). See also Philo, *On the Creation* 59 (165).

[4]Philo, *Questions and Answers on Genesis* 1.33.

[5]Ibid, 1.34.

[6]Mishnah ʾAbot 1.5.

[7]Babylonian Talmud *Menahot* 43b. Some have argued this prayer is less harsh than it sounds. The man is blessed because he has the opportunity to study Torah, an opportunity that heathens, women and slaves do not have. It is more about privilege than inherent superiority.

[8]See Mark L. Strauss, *Truth and Error in the Da Vinci Code* (San Diego: Alethinos Books, 2006), 61-70.

[9]Mt 26:6-13; 27:56, 61; 28:1; Mk 15:40, 47; 16:1; Lk 7:36-50; 8:2; 24:10; Jn 7:53–8:11; 12:1-8; 19:25; 20:1-18. The confusion can be traced back to a sermon preached by Pope Gregory the Great in the late sixth century, where he concluded that these various women were all one and the same Mary (Homily 33, in *Homiliarum in evangelia*, libri 2, *Patrologia Latina* 76 [Paris: J.-P. Migne, 1844-1864], col. 1239).

[10]For the standard exposition of this view, see *Recovering Biblical Manhood and Womanhood: A Response to Evangelical Feminism,* ed. John Piper and Wayne Grudem (Wheaton, IL: Crossway, 2012).

[11]For a thorough defense of egalitarianism, see *Discovering Biblical Equality: Complementarity Without Hierarchy,* ed. Ronald W. Pierce, Rebecca Merrill Groothuis and Gordon D. Fee (Downers Grove, IL: IVP Academic, 2005).

[12]The twelve tribes of Israel were actually thirteen, since Joseph's sons Manasseh and Ephraim became distinct tribes. Yet since Levi, as the priestly tribe, did not have an inheritance in the land, the number of tribal divisions remained twelve.

[13]I discuss this in more detail in my book *How to Read the Bible in Changing*

Times (Grand Rapids: Baker, 2011), 238-42, and in the article, "Is There Such a Thing as a Complegalitarian?," *Church Leaders*, accessed March 30, 2015, www.churchleaders.com/pastors/pastor-articles/138365-is -there-such-a-thing-as-a-complegalitarian.html.

CHAPTER 10: WAS JESUS ANTI-SEMITIC?

[1]Martin Luther, "Warning Against the Jews" (1546), in *Dr. Martin Luther's Sämmtliche Schriften*, ed. J. G. Walch (St. Louis: Concordia, 1883), 12:1264-67.

[2]Robert Michael, *Holy Hatred: Christianity, Antisemitism, and the Holocaust* (New York: Palgrave Macmillan, 2006); Robert Michael, "Luther, Luther Scholars, and the Jews," *Encounter* 46, no. 4 (Autumn 1985): 339-56.

[3]A possible exception is Matthew 28:15: "this story [of the stolen body of Jesus] has been widely circulated among *the Jews* to this very day." But this is describing conflicts that arose later in the church.

[4]Acts 13:45; 14:1-5, 19; 17:4-5, 13; 18:12; 20:3; 21:20-21, 27; 23:12; 24:5-9; 25:7.

[5]Suetonius, *Twelve Caesars, Claudius* 25.4.

CHAPTER 11: FAILED PROPHET OR VICTORIOUS KING?

[1]See Everett N. Dick, *William Miller and the Advent Crisis* (Berrien Springs, MI: Andrews University Press, 1994); George R. Knight, *Millennial Fever and the End of the World* (Boise: Pacific Press, 1993).

[2]For a history of apocalyptic and millennial movements, see Richard Kyle, *The Last Days Are Here Again: A History of the End Times* (Grand Rapids: Baker, 1998).

[3]Albert Schweitzer, *The Quest of the Historical Jesus: A Critical Study of Its Progress from Reimarus to Wrede*, trans. W. Montgomery (1906; repr., New York: Macmillan, 1954), 370-71.

[4]Bart D. Ehrman, *Jesus: Apocalyptic Prophet of the New Millennium* (Oxford: Oxford University Press, 1999), 243.

[5]False prophet: Mk 14:65; Lk 7:39; breaking the Sabbath: Mk 2:23-28//Mt 12:1-8//Lk 6:1-5; Mk 3:1-6//Mt 12:9-14//Lk 6:6-11; Lk 13:10-17; 14:1-6; Jn 5:1-18; 7:19-24; casting out demons by Satan's power: Mk 3:22-27//Mt 12:25-29//Lk 11:14-22; blasphemy: Mk 2:7//Mt 9:3//Lk 5:21; Mk 14:63-64; Lk 22:70-71; Jn 10:33.

[6]Mk 6:4//Lk 4:24//Jn 4:44; Mk 12:1-11//Mt 21:33-46//Lk 20:9-19; Mt 5:12; 13:57; 23:29-39; Lk 6:23, 26; Lk 11:47-50; 13:33-35.

[7]Gen 5:24; 1 Sam 28:1-25; 2 Kings 2:11; Job 19:25-27; Ps 16:10; 49:15; 73:24; Is 25:8; 26:19; 53:11; Ezek 37.

[8]See Is 13:10; 24:23; Ezek 32:7; Amos 5:20; 8:9; Joel 2:10; 3:15; Zeph 1:15; Rev 6:12; 8:12.

[9]1 Cor 15:23; 1 Thess 2:19; 4:15; 5:23; 2 Thess 2:1, 8; 2 Pet 3:4, 12. See also 1 Cor 11:26; 15:52; 16:22; 2 Thess 1:7; Rev 1:7; 22:7, 12, 20.

[10]C. E. B. Cranfield, *The Gospel According to Saint Mark*, rev. ed. (Cambridge: Cambridge University Press, 1977), 500.

[11]For more details, see Mark L. Strauss, *Mark*, Zondervan Exegetical Commentary on the New Testament (Grand Rapids: Zondervan, 2014), 564-67.

[12]Mt 22:44; 26:64; Mk 12:36; 14:62; Lk 20:42-43; 22:69; Acts 2:34; 5:31; 7:56; Rom 8:34; 1 Cor 15:25; Eph 1:20; Col 3:1; Heb 1:3, 13; 8:1; 10:12-13; 1 Pet 3:22; Rev 3:21; cf. Heb 5:6; 7:17, 21.

[13]Ironically, this reference has sometimes been used to try to calculate the return of Christ! See Richard Kyle, *The Last Days Are Here Again: A History of the End Times* (Grand Rapids: Baker, 1998), 36-37.

CHAPTER 12: DECAYING CORPSE OR RESURRECTED LORD?

[1]See the following debates: John Dominic Crossan and N. T. Wright, *The Resurrection of Jesus: John Dominic Crossan and N. T. Wright in Dialogue* (Minneapolis: Fortress, 2005); Paul Copan and Ronald K. Tacelli, eds., *Jesus' Resurrection: Fact or Figment? A Debate Between William Lane Craig & Gerd Lüdemann* (Downers Grove, IL: IVP Academic, 2000); Gary Habermas and Antony G. N. Flew, *Did Jesus Rise from the Dead? The Resurrection Debate* (New York: HarperCollins, 1987).

[2]For details, see my commentary *Mark*, Zondervan Exegetical Commentary (Grand Rapids: Zondervan, 2014), 714-23, or almost any commentary on Mark.

[3]For a harmonistic overview of the resurrection appearances see my textbook *Four Portraits, One Jesus: A Survey of Jesus and the Gospels* (Grand Rapids: Zondervan, 2007), 513.

[4]Bart D. Ehrman, *Jesus: Apocalyptic Prophet of the New Millennium* (Oxford: Oxford University Press, 1999), 228.

[5]Bart Ehrman, *Jesus, Interrupted: Revealing the Hidden Contradictions in the Bible* (New York: HarperOne, 2009), 175-76.

[6]David Hume, *An Enquiry Concerning Human Understanding*, ed. L. A. Selby-Bigge, 3rd ed. (Oxford: Clarendon Press, 1975).

[7]Craig S. Keener, *Miracles: The Credibility of the New Testament Accounts* (Grand Rapids: Baker Academic, 2011), 1:108.

[8]Ibid., 1:1-6.

[9]For an interesting account of surviving crucifixion, see Josephus, *Life of Flavius Josephus* 75 §420-21. During the siege of Jerusalem, Josephus sees three friends on crosses and entreats the Roman general Titus to have them taken down. Titus agrees and places them in the care of physicians, but two of the three subsequently die. Of course, this is not a botched crucifixion but an aborted one. The fact that two of the three die anyway merely confirms that Jesus would have been in no condition to proclaim his victory over death.

[10]Ehrman, *Jesus, Interrupted*, 178.

[11]Josephus, *Antiquities of the Jews* 18.3.3 §§63-64; Tacitus, *Annales ab Excessu Divi Augusti* 15.44.

[12]See John Dominic Crossan, *Jesus: A Revolutionary Biography* (San Francisco: HarperSanFrancisco, 1994), 123-58.

[13]David Friedrich Strauss, *The Life of Jesus Critically Examined*, trans. George Eliot and ed. Peter C. Hodgson (Philadelphia: Fortress, 1972), 739.

[14]Gerd Lüdemann, *What Really Happened to Jesus?*, trans. John Bowden (Louisville: Westminster John Knox, 1993), 80.

[15]Paula Fredriksen, *From Jesus to Christ* (New Haven, CT: Yale University Press, 2000), 133.

[16]E. P. Sanders, *The Historical Figure of Jesus* (New York: Penguin, 1993), 280.

[17]I say "tend to" because some visions and apparitions have been reported as quite real and even physical. For an interesting discussion of similarities and differences between apparitions of the dead and the resurrection appearances, see Dale Allison, *Resurrecting Jesus: The Earliest Christian Tradition and Its Interpreters* (New York: T&T Clark, 2005).

[18]N. T. Wright, *The Resurrection of the Son of God* (Minneapolis: Fortress, 2003), 686-96.

[19]Craig S. Keener, *The Historical Jesus of the Gospels* (Grand Rapids: Eerdmans, 2012), 342.

Scripture Index

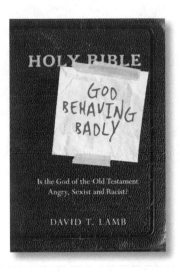

God Behaving Badly
David. T. Lamb
ISBN 978-0-8308-3826-4 (print)
ISBN 978-0-8308-6869-8 (digital)